Table of Contents

Preface

It is now almost 20 years since we started coming from Vancouver, BC twice a year to vacation in Arizona, time enough to notice many changes: more people, more developments, additional trails. The city of Payson has grown beyond our expectations, and the realignment and 4-laning of the Beeline Highway (State Route 87) and State Route 260 east of Payson to the Rim have made travel to the area from Phoenix and from towns on the Rim much shorter and easier.

This area was chosen because there was no comprehensive description of the Highline Trail (a National Recreational Trail of historic significance) and its side-trails. Part of the Mazatzal Mountain range is reachable from the Payson area for day hikes, but there are already two guidebooks covering that area[1], so we have only included the most scenic and popular hike, the Barnhardt Trail, and two trails near SR 87 in the Deer Creek area.

All lands in this guidebook are under Forest Service management, mostly in the Tonto National Forest, with a few extending a bit above the Rim into the Coconino or Sitgreaves National Forests. Tonto National Forest staff have collaborated in this project, but are not responsible for the accuracy of each description.

The actual field work has extended over 10 years.

Many of the trails were developed for use by horses, or simply by informal horse usage. We address this guidebook to equestrians as well as hikers, runners, and more recently, mountain-bikers. Generally we have not attempted to specify the appropriateness of a particular trail's usage except insofar as "hiker only" trails have been so designated by the Forest Service, or indirectly by means of descriptions of steepness, loose rock, etc.

Some system trails have unsigned and therefore confusing junctions. We have dealt with this problem by giving a general description with major distances to the tenth of a mile, followed in most cases by a very detailed tabular description to the hundredth of a mile, meant only for actual use on the trail. Since some of these trails were first measured, new junctions with non-system (nondesignated) trails may be present, and a few have been deleted.

The Dude Fire and subsequent forest fires related to the prolonged area drought have changed – and may further change – trail conditions. Heavy beetle-kill of many sections of forest are creating greater risk of extensive fires. Under new laws, selective thinning of dense tree stands and salvage logging of recently killed trees have already started. In the summer of 2004 a devastating fire burned much of the Mazatzal Wilderness. *It shouldn't be necessary to emphasize that smoking in the forest, throwing cigarette butts out of car windows, and carelessness with fires and stoves can have devastating effects.* Be aware that trail descriptions in this book are subject to change, and be prepared to be in the mountains longer than you may have expected.

---

[1] David Mazel's *Arizona Trails, 3rd edition,* 1989. Berkeley, CA: Wilderness Press, and Bruce Grubbs' *Hiking Arizona's Superstition & Mazatzal Country.* 2000. Helena, MT: Falcon Publishing.

You may wonder why the General George Crook Trail near the edge of the Rim is not included in the trail descriptions or shown in red on the maps. This is because the trail location is approximate only, frequently intersecting as it does the roads near the Rim and having no clear, continuous trailway. The special chevron marking is of the route only, despite its being designating a National Recreation Trail. Its approximate location is shown on our maps in black.

Because the format of the guide requires coordination of general (narrative) descriptions, tabular (detailed) descriptions, and maps, it is important to read the section *How to Use This Guide. Suggestions for Hikers* also has some essential pointers.

Maps are in two colors, so to minimize costs it was necessary to print and bind them together in one section, rather than with their trail descriptions.

A few words must be said about responsibility. While we have taken every precaution of which we are aware to obtain and publish accurate information and to collaborate with agency staff, there are some limitations of which you should be aware:

(1)   There is no guarantee of complete accuracy.
(2)   Although Forest Service staff have seen the maps and reviewed the text at various points, no official endorsement is implied or should be assumed.
(3)   Trails may change due to erosion, weather, usage patterns, and agency policy. Most are not regularly maintained or patrolled on the ground, and many are not signed or marked. Some are rough and steep. It is not difficult to become confused or lost, or to twist an ankle. The whole point of hiking or riding in the mountains is to get away from a city-like atmosphere. So enjoy your excursion, *but realize that you are accepting the risks entailed.*

You can help maintain the accuracy and usefulness of this guide. If you become aware of errors or changes, let us know *at the address below.* You may use the correction form at the back of this book. The responsible agency should also be informed.

Roger & Ethel Freeman, Box 2033, Point Roberts, WA 98281
E-mail: rfreeman@cw.bc.ca
Phone (604) 263-3900
Web site for up-dates: www.freemanbooks.com

Acknowledgements

This book would never have been written without the assistance of others.

We would like to thank our publisher, Al Mayerski of Gem Guides, and his editor, Nancy Fox and later Kathy Mayerski, for their unfailing support. Our cartographer, Angus Weller, has maintained his good cheer while providing high-quality output despite varying deadlines and inputs from us.

Our special thanks go to Tonto National Forest staff. In particular, Walt Thole of the Payson District office met with us regularly, collaborated in information collection, sometimes dropped us off at remote trailheads we could not reach in our rental vehicle, and throughout was kind, warm-hearted and patient. "Pete" Weinel of the National Forest office in Phoenix has been a gold mine of information about history and policies affecting trails and has always been available when we needed his help. He has since retired and we wish him a happy and fulfilling life.

We have also met at least once with staff from the Tonto Basin and Mesa Forest Districts, and as members of the Gila County Trails Alliance have met with other members.

We would be remiss if we failed to mention our friends Del Seppanen, formerly with the City of Phoenix Parks, Recreation & Library Department, and his wife Mary, who for many years have stored our equipment in their home and offered friendship and a "home away from home" in our Arizona travels.

How to Use This Book

General Advice

Since the tabular descriptions are very detailed, *it is very important to read the following section* to understand how these relate to the general descriptions and maps. Although we have provided trail maps and access information, there is no substitute for full road maps; we advise that you obtain a good one and have the Tonto National Forest map available, too.

Trail Areas, Indicators, and Features

Each major trail has a text (and map) indicator. These are usually the official Forest Service number (and sometimes the name).

We have been impressed with the many changes and improvements that have taken place. *But it has been impossible to check every trail again over our 10-year period of field work.* (We would appreciate hearing about these changes.)

Matching Book Descriptions and the Maps

Maps are in a separate section at the back of the book (to save costs of color printing). Each has its number outside the map border in the upper outside corner, as well as a name in capitals on the map. There is an index map.

Each trail section indicates the map number(s) and name(s). *Trails indicated in black* are either partly on private land or for other reasons regarded as closed, undesignated, undesirable, impossible to follow, or of no significance. They are shown only to eliminate confusion at trail junctions and for safety reasons; please do *not* regard their inclusion as a recommendation for use.

Abbreviations Used in Tabular Descriptions

L = left	N = north	NE = northeast	SE = southeast
R = right	S = south	NW = northwest	SW = southwest
mi = mile	FR = Forest Rd	SR = State Route	4WD = 4 wheel drive
NDT = non-designated trail		elev. = elevation	TH = trailhead
CG = campground			

Similarly, "sharp L," "half-L" and "W-bound" should be self-explanatory.

Using the Detailed Tabular Descriptions

The reverse or "Read Up" column on the right of the tabular descriptions serves as a useful source of information when traveling in the direction of the description: it indicates how far you still have to go. The descriptions themselves have to be reversed mentally for travel in the opposite direction.

For example:

Read Down ↓	Detailed Trail Description	Read Up ↑
0.00	From trailhead, head NW (1,480').	0.57
0.49	Keep L, approach canal.	0.08
0.55	**Junction:** join trail from R; parallel canal fence.	0.02
0.57	**Junction:** trail R descends to canal and can be followed to 1.49 mi and beyond.	0.00

Note that in reading *up*, "L" becomes "R" and vice versa, and "ascend" becomes "descend." (It may take a bit of practice to get used to this.)

Distances in General and in Detailed Descriptions

For the sake of simplicity, measured distances in the *general descriptions* have been truncated to the nearest tenth or quarter of a mile, for example 0.14 → 0.1 and 0.23 → 0.25. In the detailed descriptions, distances are given to the nearest hundredth of a mile (0.01 mi = 52.8').

Suggestions for Hikers

With the Assistance of L. V. Yates, Jr.

The following hints are not meant to be exhaustive or definitive. (Detailed information is available in sources listed in the Bibliography, Appendix C). This chapter is a modification of that in our first Arizona book, *Day Hikes and Trail Rides In and Around Phoenix, 2nd edition*, 2000, also published by Gem Guides.

Everyone has different views on what is important in hiking. The season of the year, age, experience and size of party, elevation and length of trip all can create highly variable circumstances for which it is difficult to make general pronouncements. Seasoned hikers tend to be highly individualistic and therefore the ideas expressed here are mostly intended for the novice.

Safety

♦ Leave word about your start, destination, and estimated time of return with someone reliable. If rescue is required, contact the County Sheriff's office, whose job it is to call out the rescue team.

♦ Large groups tend to separate into slow and fast hikers. Periodically check on your party, and have an experienced person bring up the rear. <u>*Do not travel alone, especially in the back-country*</u>.

♦ *Be prepared for changes in the weather.* The return route and familiar landmarks may become obscure or confusing when weather conditions change. Take extra clothing on moderate to long hikes. Remember that the Rim "makes its own weather."

♦ *Be prepared for injury* (bring first-aid material) *and for getting lost* (bring some food and ample water). Pack a flashlight and extra batteries.

♦ Don't roll rocks down steep slopes or cliffs. Someone may be below.

♦ In summer, flash floods may occur in normally dry washes. If thunderstorms are in the area, descend from elevated areas to avoid lightning.

♦ Poisonous reptiles and insects live in the desert and mountains. You are unlikely to have trouble if you only put your hands and feet in places you can see.

♦ The spines of some types of cactus, especially the "jumping" cholla, are very easy to collect in your skin, even through your shoes. Carry a comb and strong tweezers or long-nose pliers to remove them.

Comfort

♦ Rule #1 is: **_bring sufficient water_**. *This cannot be overemphasized.*

* Wear comfortable clothing; use a hat, sunscreen and sunglasses.
* If you are not experienced and fit, take short hikes before long ones. This will give you a chance to assess your fitness and break in hiking boots. Bring an extra pair of socks. Treat potential blisters before they become major problems (carry moleskin, readjust socks when you rest).
* Insects are not generally a problem, but at certain times (especially near dusk) there may be mosquitoes, large and small flies, spiders, and even Africanized bees. Bring repellent, and of course your medicine if you are subject to severe reactions from specific stinging insects.
* Leave valuables at home. The next best place is in the trunk of your car.
* Take a spare car key and remember to turn off your headlights!

Mountain Ethics

Most of us enjoy hiking not only for exercise, but for the closer contact we feel with nature. *A respectful attitude to man and nature* makes many of these recommendations redundant: the ideas are then mostly "common sense."

* Flowers, rocks, and other "specimens" should be left in place. The best guide is "take nothing but pictures, leave nothing but footprints." An exception is garbage thoughtlessly left by others. This you *can* take out!
* Keep to the trails — *please do not cut across switchbacks* — it will contribute to the trail's eventual destruction through erosion.
* Do not remove markers, signs, or cairns — they are not souvenirs. Someone's safety or life could depend upon them.
* Please do not deface the trees and rocks with graffiti. It is especially important to respect aboriginal petroglyphs if you come across them.
* *"Pack it in — pack it out" applies to everything.* Orange peels, candy wrappers, pop bottles or cans are unsightly and non-biodegradable. Bury no refuse — animals will dig it up.
* If you smoke on the trail, be especially careful in disposing of cigarettes and matches.
* Respect private property.
* Other users of the mountains will be grateful if you avoid creating unnecessarily loud noises (for example, with "boom boxes").
* Use of trail-bikes or other motorized all-terrain vehicles off designated highways or forest roads in the National Forests is prohibited. Bicycles are not allowed in wilderness areas, and certain trails leading to wilderness area boundaries may be posted with restrictions. Report problems to the responsible managing agency.
* Your dog deserves comfort and safety, too — at home!

Weather

With an annual rainfall of 20.7 inches (Phoenix gets 7.5"), Payson is often sunny, especially in the months of April through June. July and August get the most precipitation; September and December through March receive about 2 inches each. Snow falls in winter at times, especially on the Rim. (After the snow melts, the plateau beyond the Rim can be very muddy and unpaved roads may be impassable.) Afternoon and evening thundershowers are common between July and September, and moist air (a true monsoon) may be sucked up from the Gulfs of Mexico or California as far as Payson, though less frequently than in the Phoenix area. Payson has average temperatures of 5_ lower than Phoenix, the Rim much lower still. From November through March, nights are cold.

Below is a table of the average daily temperatures for Payson for each month:

Month	Average Daily Maximum	Average Daily Minimum
January	60.1°	31.5°
February	65.3°	34.6°
March	70.4°	38.2°
April	78.8°	43.9°
May	88.4°	51.3°
June	98.3°	59.0°
July	102.0°	67.8°
August	99.1°	66.1°
September	94.3°	59.6°
October	84.2°	48.4°
November	70.8°	37.8°
December	60.9°	32.7°

Despite the high temperatures in summer, one can usually hike and ride if precautions are taken:

♦ On days expected to be very hot, go very early in the morning, wear protective clothing (a hat, sunscreen, and light clothing), and bring *plenty* of water (at least a gallon if you will be out all day).

♦ If you are new to the area or have any health problems, start out with very short trips and build up endurance slowly.

Because of the warmth, there is a temptation to hike or ride in shorts and a short-sleeved shirt and not to bring clothing to cover arms and legs — this is a dangerous mistake. Severe sunburn occurs easily during summer months, but may occur at any time of the year, especially in those with light complexions. Heat exhaustion may be prevented by taking enough fluid and resting periodically in the shade.

Cool weather in combination with fatigue and wet, windy conditions may lead to hypothermia (dangerous lowering of the body's central core temperature). Due to impaired judgment, the impending hazard may not be accurately perceived.

History

The Mogollon Rim is an impressive natural feature, stretching from the Red Rock Country near Sedona on the west into New Mexico on the east. The elevation changes abruptly from over 8,000' on parts of the Rim to 6,000' below.

Cowboys and Indians, homesteaders, prospectors, ranchers and soldiers were part of the area's history, much of which has unfortunately been lost or was never recorded. The jumbled terrain, lack of easy access, and frontier clashes between natives and non-natives made early settling hazardous. The area was much affected by the skirmishes that took place, largely responses of the Federal government to the insecurity felt by settlers, particularly toward the Apaches after the Civil War.

General George Crook was appointed to pacify or fight the Apaches, and built a road along the Rim between Fort McDowell and Fort Verde, the route of which is now marked (but it is not a continuous trailway). General George Stoneman was sent out to deal more ruthlessly with raiding Apache bands, since General Crook was thought to be too lenient and understanding.

Al Sieber, famed Indian scout, roamed north of Globe, but probably not as far north as Payson.

Early settler families included the following whose names will be found in the area: Barnhart, Childs, Chilson, Christopher, Cline, Derrick, Drew, Ellison, Haught, Horton, Houston, Roberts, Star[r], and Webber.

"Mazatzal," pronounced in several different ways, is said to derive from an Indian word for "rugged" or "barren."

Roads into the area were primitive until fairly recently. Anyone driving from Phoenix to Payson can easily see why, as the highway crosses several steep mountain ranges and valleys. The way down the Rim to Strawberry was especially hazardous. Major road improvements have made day trips from Phoenix a reality, and a rapidly expanding population keeps pressure on the Forest Service to provide and maintain trails and trail information, and to minimize garbage, vandalism, fire risks and consequences, and user conflicts. The magnitude of these tasks merits our respect.

History is being made today, as drought, beetle infestations, and fire alter the terrain that trails cross and the scenic panoramas that recreationists seek.

The Highline Trail origin is still in dispute. Part of it was thought to be a native route, and part probably was built by settlers or established by their use in dispersed areas.

Further history can be gleaned from books listed in Appendix C and by visiting the Payson Library.

Introduction to the Tonto National Forest

The Mogollon Rim is one of the most significant landmarks of the Tonto National Forest, one of the largest National Forests in the continental United States. It embraces nearly 3 million acres (1.1 million hectares) of rugged scenic landscapes, ranging from the cactus-studded deserts to the pine-clad mountains. The Tonto is also one of the most visited, and is truly one of "America's Great Outdoors."[*]

In addition to its outstanding recreational opportunities, the Tonto National Forest is a repository of clean water, diverse wildlife habitats, and many historic and prehistoric sites. Grazing by domestic livestock, timber harvesting, and prospecting for minerals are also components of the multiple-use management policy mandated by Congress. Its scenic beauty is also considered an important resource, but is one of the most difficult to protect, due to all of the man-made impacts upon it.

Present evidence indicates that the area was one of the earliest occupied in Arizona: it supported a variety of settlements and groups almost continuously for 11,000 years. Two present-day Indian groups settled within the Tonto area. This Forest also is home to the Pinal and Tonto Apache, some bands of San Carlos and Cibecue Apache, and the Fort McDowell Yavapai. Many years later (the 1820s), Kit Carson's group was one of the first non-Indian groups to visit this general area.

After the Civil War, the Federal government renew its interest in this remote country and established a few army posts throughout the Arizona Territory. Troops scouted throughout this area in the late 1860s and 1870s. A few prospectors, traders, packers, and other adventurous characters visited the Tonto Basin and returned with stories of the fine grasses and ideal climate. Cattlemen, always anxious to find newer ranges, began bringing herds of cattle beginning in the 1870s. As more and more people found this area, small towns were created such as Maryville, Pine, and Payson. In 1898, the Mogollon Rim area was designed the Black Mesa Forest Reserve; in 1908, several Forest Reserves were grouped into the Tonto National Forest, and a few Forest Rangers began to do their best to properly manage this area. Four years later, this area became part of the new State of Arizona.

More and more people poured into Arizona: towns became cities, and more than one city has become a megalopolis. The impacts on natural resources increased every year, as did problems between users. These problems remain with us today. It became more and more difficult for the Forest Service to protect natural resources while serving visitors.

Some people ignore laws and regulations which protect other visitors and the National Forests themselves. Action had to be taken to control their activities,

---

[*]National Recreation Strategy, 1988

but prohibitions and other actions unfortunately also affect visitors who fully appreciate their public lands. Despite these types of concerns, the Mogollon Rim is one of the most enjoyed areas in Arizona. Now, in a single day, hundreds of people visit and recreate at this very special place.

There is a wide spectrum of recreation opportunities. Sightseeing, fishing, hunting, photography, hiking, horseback riding, biking, 4-wheeling, camping, and picnicking are all popular. There are more than six developed recreation sites for camping and/or picnicking within this part of the Forest. One of these developed recreation sites is for groups who have reserved use of it on a specific day. There is also a brand-new campground recently built. There are certified guides who take people out for hiking, horseback riding, or hunting (check in at the Local Ranger Station to be sure the guide is authorized).

There are also more than six trailheads for parking so that people can seek out a variety of trails. Approximately 85 miles (144 km) of National Forest System Trails are available, as well as many miles of National Forest System Roads. The Highline Trail has been designated a National Recreation Trail by the Chief of the Forest Service, USDA. Parts of several trails have also been designated sections of the Arizona Trail.

Some of the trails in this area are in very good condition, but others are in <u>bad</u> shape. These trails vary from an easy loop-hike near a trailhead, to a steep and rocky trail only suitable for an experienced backcountry hiker or equestrian. Some trails are <u>not</u> even recommended for horses. (Do not take your horse there without finding out about the situation to be faced.)

Remember: this is not a city park. Everyone intending to use these trails is responsible for personally assessing these conditions, as well as his or her own ability to cope with them. Please be aware that all recreational hiking and horseback-riding involves a degree of risk, and persons engaged in this activity assume the risk associated therewith.

Guidebooks can be a well of information, and tell you much about specific trails. A good guidebook must not only be user-friendly, it must also be accurate when written, and revised regularly to be kept accurate. In the years I have worked with Roger and Ethel Freeman, they have shown that their standards are high, and that they can both produce and update excellent trail guidebooks. I'm sure that many people will benefit from their efforts.

You are welcome to use our trails, recognizing that the Forest Service is unable to maintain them as well as we would like. If you encounter a particular problem on the trail or need additional information, you are very welcome to contact one of our offices (see Appendix B for addresses and phone numbers).

Pete Weinel, Assistant Group Leader for Public Service, USDA Forest Service

Easy, Attractive Hikes

If you're just starting out in the area, have little time, or you are hiking with small children, the following hikes may be worth considering. *Be aware that recent insect kill and fires may have caused trail changes.*

When travelling with children, remember to carry a tweezers or small pliers to deal with any cactus they may encounter, and be careful near lake and cliff areas.

Area	Section, Name	Pages	Map	Comments
Rim	Rim Lakes Vista Trail	134	17	Mountain views, partially paved; use *extreme care* in some areas where edge is not fenced
Pine Trailhead	Highline Trail to Pineview; Pine Canyon back to TH	38, 82, 85	2	Easy walking, varied, some views
Highline Trail	W of Tonto Creek	68	12	Good views; can loop with FR 289C & FR 289
Horton Creek	First 1.5 miles, Horton Creek Trail	104	13, 14	Beautiful riparian area, falls
Pine Creek Loop	Pine Creek Loop	143	25	Mountain views; highly recommended
Fossil Creek	Flume Trail	125	20	Initial rough ascent to service road
Mazatzals	Barnhardt Trail, first part	135	23	Spectacular views in first mile; further on extreme care must be used on cliffs
Mazatzals	South Fork Trail, Deer Creek	138	24	Lower portion has beautiful flats and old stone cabin ruin

Highline Trail Tabular Summary

Mileage W → E Read Down	Reference Point	Mileage E → W Read Up
0.00	**Pine Trailhead, SR 87**	**50.51**
0.06	Pine Canyon Trail [26]	50.45
1.10	Pineview Trail [28]	49.41
1.55	Donahue Trail [27]	48.96
3.58	Red Rock Spring Trail [294]	46.93
7.68	Geronimo Trail [240]	42.83
8.04	**FR 440 (Camp Geronimo)**	**42.47**
9.94	Poison Spring Trail [29]	40.57
17.26	Col Devin Trail [290]	33.25
17.31	**FR 32A (Washington Park)**	**33.20**
17.54	Pump House Trail [296]	32.97
23.82	FR 144 (4WD only)	26.69
25.72	Myrtle Trail [30]	24.79
32.81	FR 289C	17.70
33.40	**FR 289 (Tonto Creek)**	**17.11**
36.81	Horton Creek Trail [292]	13.70
36.84	Horton Springs Trail	13.67
38.49	Promontory Trail [site]	12.02
39.78	Derrick Trail [33]	10.73
44.15	**FR 284 (Christopher Creek)**	**6.36**
44.32	See Canyon Trail [184]	6.19
46.39	Drew Trail [291]	4.12
50.51	**260 Trailhead near SR 260**	**0.00**

The Highline Trail

Trail Descriptions

Direction:

WEST to EAST

[31] Highline Trail WEST to EAST

Pine Trailhead to Geronimo Trailhead [FR 440]

Introduction. The Highline Trail starts from a good trailhead with ample parking, a corral and toilet, and offers a varied and long walk along the flank of the Rim for 8 miles to FR 440 near Camp Geronimo. The trip can be broken by side-trails at several points. In places the footway is rough, and careful planning is needed for through trips on foot.

Maps. *Our Maps 2, 3 & 5 (Highline 2: Pine, Highline 3: Milk Ranch Point,* and *Highline 5: Camp Geronimo).* The USGS 1:24,000 Pine quadrangle (1973) covers the terrain but shows only part of the trail and none of its side-trails. The Tonto National Forest map (2001) shows this section.

Access. *At the western end,* from SR 87, 0.5 mile south of Pine or 14.2 miles north of the junction of SR 87 and SR 260 in Payson, take a paved road 0.2 mile to the trailhead at a sign. *At the eastern end,* from FR 440, 2 miles north of the Control Road [FR 64]. The Pine Trailhead area was heavily damaged by beetle infestations and was selectively logged in 2003.

General Description. The trail leaves the parking area at a sign, ascending easily to a junction at 0.1 mile where the Pine Canyon Trail [26] goes left. Ascending through pine forest, the Highline Trail follows up a creek to the Pineview Trail [28] at 1.1 miles. It crosses the creek and ascends, with some views, to the Donahue Trail [27] at 1.6 miles. The trail ascends 450' in 2/3 of a mile, with good views. It then goes up and down along the flank of the Rim to Red Rock Spring and the Red Rock Spring Trail [294] at 3.6 miles. Beyond, the trail continues up and down along the flank, passing Pine Spring at 4.7 miles, offering increasing views of the Webber Creek valley, and crosses the creek to Geronimo Trailhead at 8 miles. Total elevation gain is 1,280'. (Note: Webber Creek can be difficult to cross after wet weather.)

Read Down ↓	Detailed Trail Description	Read Up ↑
0.00	From Pine Trailhead at 5,400', the trail ascends gradually through conifers.	8.04
0.03	Pass thru gate in barbed-wire fence.	8.01
0.05	Ascend steadily to the R.	7.99
0.06	**Junction:** on L is Pine Canyon Trail [26]. On it 0.5 mi is the junction with the Pineview Trail [28]. Continue to the R.	7.98
0.10	Descend, with stock tank below on R.	7.94
0.15	Bottom of descent, with trail sharp R (back to stock tank) just before this point. Ascend.	7.89
0.42	Level off (5,500').	7.62
0.82	Cross creek, ascend R, parallelling it.	7.22
0.90	Top of rise; descend gradually to creek.	7.14
0.97	Edge of creek, bear L, crossing rocky area.	7.07
1.10	**Junction:** just before a crossing of the creek, in a small open area, sharp L is the Pineview Trail [28] to Pine Canyon Trail [26] in 0.65 mi. The Highline Trail continues to the E, crossing the creek (5,720').	6.94
1.26	**Junction:** on R is poor vehicleway just before barbed-wire fence; there are 2 more connections with this vehicleway in the next few feet.	6.78

1.41 Switchback to L (N). Beyond, there is a trenched section. 6.63
1.51 Switchback to L, then head E. 6.53
1.55 **Junction:** Donahue Trail [27] turns L here; to Milk Ranch Point in 1.1 mi;
      to FR 218 in 2.6 mi. Elevation here 5,880'. The Highline Trail continues E,
      going briefly up and down. 6.49
1.64 Bottom of descent. 6.40
1.68 Enter forest. 6.36
1.69 Start ascent (5,860'). 6.35
1.72 Switchback to R. 6.32
1.73 Turn L. 6.31
1.77 Bear R, then R again in 250'. 6.27
1.87 Switchback to L (S). Elevation 6,010'). Ascend steadily. 6.17
1.91 Switchback to R, then to L in 100'. 6.13
1.98 Switchback to R, ascend toward crest. 6.06
2.02 Turn L onto crest [on reverse, use care to find spot where trail leaves crest].
      Elevation 6,160'). Ascend crest of subsidiary ridge, with views. 6.02
2.06 Ease grade of ascent. This is a scenic area. 5.98
2.09 Leave crest to L of it, ascending gradually. 5.95
2.13 Turn R (E), ascend. 5.91
2.15 Top of rise on subsidiary ridge (6,250'), cross over and descend, then ascend. ... 5.89
2.24 Top of rise, good viewpoint (6,310'). 5.80
2.28 Top of rise (6,270'). Views expand in open area. 5.76
2.37 Top of rise (6,220'). 5.67
2.48 Bottom of descent. 5.56
2.52 Top of rise (6,190'). 5.52
2.58 Cross main branch of creek in broad, pleasant valley (6,150'). 5.46
2.68 Turn R, ascend out of valley. 5.36
2.69 Switchback to L, then to R in 100'. 5.35
2.76 Reach top of climb out of valley. Ascend gradually. 5.28
2.88 Top of rise in attractive area (6,220'). 5.16
2.91 Start steady descent. 5.13
2.99 Ease descent briefly. 5.05
3.00 Cross small sag. 5.04
3.02 Top of rise. 5.02
3.07 Top of rise; views. 4.97
3.19 Small sag. 4.85
3.21 Top of rise (6,040'). 4.83
3.25 Top of rise. 4.79
3.29 Cross creek in valley (6,020'). 4.75
3.32 Cross sag. Ascend steadily out of it. 4.72
3.43 Top of rise (6,080'). 4.61
3.49 Spring. 4.55
3.51 Red Rock Spring area [sign]. 70' beyond is a seep. 4.53
3.55 Box spring for stock on R. Descend gradually W. 4.49
3.58 **Junction:** on R is the Red Rock Spring Trail [294], leading down 1 mi to
      Control Road [FR 64], 2.5 mi E of SR 87. Elevation 6,000'. Continue E,
      descending. 4.46
3.73 Bottom of descent. 4.31
3.76 Descend again, to N. 4.28
3.79 Cross creek (5,900'). 4.15
3.86 Top of rise. Head E, level trail. Descend in 200', for 200'. 4.08
4.02 Cross small creek. Ascend to N. 3.92
4.04 Top of rise (5,890'). 3.90

4.20   Top of rise. Ascend N again. 3.74
4.29   Top of rise, and another in 300' (6,000'). 3.65
4.37   Cross creek and seeps. Use care in muddy, trenched area. 3.57
4.38   Top of rise; another in 200'. Descend for 200', then ascend for 100'. 3.50
4.50   Bottom of descent. 3.44
4.53   Top of rise, viewpoint. Side-hill to NW, into canyon. 3.41
4.64   Top of rise in pleasant area in the pines. Ignore game trails to L. Descend R. 3.30
4.67   Gate [open]. Pine Spring in wet area. 3.27
4.70   Cross creek with beautiful pools. Head SE. 3.24
4.76   Top of rise on crest of broad ridge (6,030'). Descend to E. 3.18
4.93   Head SE on rocky trail. 3.01
5.06   Descend to N (5,900'). 2.88
5.15   Turn to E. 2.79
5.16   Cross flood plain and wash. Rise to NE. 2.78
5.20   Top of rise (5,860'). 2.74
5.35   Cross creek. 2.59
5.38   Top of rise. Head ENE. 2.56
5.67   Cross very small wash (5,920'), ascend onto plateau. Easy walking. 2.27
5.74   Top of rise. 2.20
5.81   Views start into Webber Creek valley. Descend to NW. 2.13
5.93   Bottom of descent; level. 2.01
6.03   Descend to N. Cross small washes. 1.91
6.14   Descend to E. 1.80
6.31   Descend to S. 1.63
6.39   Switchback to L. Descend steadily to N, then swing E. 1.55
6.45   Cross small creek, ascend to N, out of forest. 1.49
6.52   Views open. Trail is well-constructed along a side-hill. 1.42
6.63   Ascend steeply N (some sections are eroding). 1.31
6.64   Pass rocks on L. 1.30
6.67   Top of rise. Very scenic route (5,740'). 1.27
6.75   Top of rise. 1.19
6.83   Top of rise. 1.11
6.86   Descend steadily to N. 1.08
6.96   Switchback to R. In 245', level out. 0.98
7.03   Switchback to R up rocky trail. 0.91
7.07   Top of rise (5,710'). 0.87
7.18   Cross creek, then 4 small ones in the next 750'. 0.76
7.40   Leave crest, descend (5,750'). 0.64
7.63   Turn L. 0.41
7.68   **Junction:** Geronimo Trail [240] sharp L (to West Webber [228], Turkey
        Springs [217], and East Webber [289] Trails). Descend to R. 0.36
7.73   Cross old vehicleway. 0.31
7.79   Cross creek. 0.21
7.86   Cross vehicleway. 0.14
7.97   **Junction:** trail of use sharp R. Continue to L. 0.07
8.01   Cross secondary branch of Webber Creek. 0.03
8.03   Cross main branch of Webber Creek. 0.01
8.04   **Junction:** FR 440 (2 mi N of Control Road [FR 64]), parking area (5,420').
        The Highline Trail continues E. 0.00

[31] Highline Trail   WEST TO EAST

FR 440 (Camp Geronimo) to FR 32A (Washington Park)

Introduction. This section of the trail has much variety. The results of the Dude Fire can be seen around Bray Creek, but most of this area was little affected. It is a long return trip on foot, really not feasible without leaving a car at one end or the other.

Maps. *Our Maps 5-7 (Highline 5: Camp Geronimo, Highline 6: N Sycamore Creek, and Highline 7: Washington Park).* The USGS 1:24,000 Kehl Ridge Quadrangle (1972) covers part of the trail, some of it in an old and now incorrect location.

Access. *At the western end,* from FR 440 at Geronimo Trailhead, 2 miles north of the Control Road [FR 64]. *At the eastern end,* from Washington Park Trailhead at the end of FR 32A.

General Description. After ascending out of the Webber Creek valley along the flank of the Rim for almost 2 miles, a spur trail [29] leads 0.5 mile to Poison Spring. Bray Creek is crossed at 3 miles and the deep ravine of North Sycamore Creek at 4.25 miles. There is then considerable up and down with occasional very fine level sections through forest. The trail descends a long slope to cross a private road and Mail Creek at 8.3 miles and the power line service road at 9 miles. There is then a final descent to meet the Col. Devin Trail [290] at 9.2 miles, just before reaching the Washington Park Trailhead at 9.25 miles. Total ascent is 1,400'.

NOTE that Camp Geronimo hosts thousands of Scouts, and over time quite a number of non-system trails have developed. Be careful to stay on the main trails.

Read Down ↓	Detailed Trail Description	Read Up ↑
0.00	From Geronimo Trailhead (5,420'), ascend immediately N.	9.27
0.11	**Junction:** trail of use sharp R.	9.16
0.14	**Junction:** trail of use L (to Camp Geronimo). Keep R.	9.13
0.16	Top of rise (5,480'). Level.	9.11
0.20	**Junction:** trail of use on L. Continue straight, ascending gradually.	9.07
0.23	**Junction:** trail of use on L. Keep R here.	9.04
0.34	Top of rise.	8.93
0.39	**Junctions:** many trails of use in this area.	8.88
0.40	Top of rise (5,580'). Dirt service road parallels trail on L. Water tank ahead.	8.87
0.49	Descend R (sign).	8.78
0.51	Cross small creek.	8.76
0.54	Start steady ascent to E & then to SE.	8.73
0.57	Switchback to L.	8.70
0.58	**Junction:** trail of use on R; keep L.	8.69
0.59	**Junction:** previous trail rejoins.	8.68
0.60	Switchback to R, then level off.	8.67
0.61	**Junction:** trail of use sharp L. Service road on L, paralleling trail.	8.66
0.65	**Junction:** keep L; then pass another on L in 30'.	8.62

0.67	**Junction (4-way):** trails of use cross. Descend gradually.	8.60
0.74	**Junction:** trail of use sharp R. Ascend steadily.	8.53
0.81	Top of rise. Descend briefly, then go up & down.	8.46
0.92	Cross (dry) creek, then ascend steeply, then moderately.	8.35
1.03	Viewpoint to R. Elevation 5,810').	8.24
1.12	Ascend, swinging N.	8.15
1.20	Top of rise.	8.07
1.21	Cross small creek.	8.06
1.25	Start steady ascent.	8.02
1.30	Cross same creek. Ascend steadily N & then NE.	7.97
1.39	**Junction:** keep R on narrower trail.	7.88
1.48	**Junction:** service road on L. Viewpoint (6,100'). Descend.	7.79
1.50	**Junction:** trail splits. Go L, descending.	7.77
1.53	Turn R; level.	7.74
1.54	Open area; use care with route-finding. Descend to E.	7.73
1.57	**Junction:** original trail descends to L; keep straight on.	7.70
1.59	Turn L, then zigzag.	7.68
1.61	Steep pitch; then reach **junction** and rejoin original route.	7.66
1.65	Bottom of descent (5,980'). Ascend to N.	7.62
1.73	Turn R (E); ease grade of ascent.	7.54
1.74	Turn to NE.	7.53
1.77	**Junction:** at top of rise and gate (Bear Spring area is on R; downhill is stock tank) BSA's Rim View Trail [undesignated] goes L (6,040').	7.50

1.79　**Junction:**　service road bears L here; sign for [31] with arrows missing.
Ascend on old vehicleway. 7.48
1.86　Top of rise; level trail toward E. 7.41
1.90　**Important junction:**　Poison Spring Trail [29] uphill on L (to Spring in 0.5 mi).
Water may not be available. Ascend wide, rocky trail. 7.37
1.95　Descend steadily into valley; spires and cliffs ahead. 7.32
2.01　Bottom of descent. 7.26
2.07　Descend into valley of Poison Spring. 7.20
2.15　Top of rise; descend. 7.12
2.16　Switchback to R and cross valley; ascend. 7.11
2.18　Top of rise. Descend briefly, then ascend NE & N. 7.09
2.30　Top of rise (6,240'). 6.97
2.31　Side-hill valley on R. 6.96
2.39　Top of rise (6,190'). Bear L and descend. 6.88
2.45　Eroded trail for 80'. 6.82
2.48　Cross wash; ascend. 6.79
2.49　Top of rise. 6.78
2.52　Descend steadily NNE briefly, then side-hill. 6.75
2.57　Turn W, ascend. 6.70
2.61　Switchback to L. 6.66
2.68　Top of rise on shoulder of ridge (6,220'). 6.59
2.72　Ascend gradually, then moderately steeply, with rock spires above on L. 6.55
2.81　Top of rise (6,310'). Descend into semi-open area. 6.46
2.84　Bottom of descent. Go up & down. 6.43
2.94　Top of rise; descend NE; enter area of Dude Fire, seen above near Rim. 6.33
2.97　Bottom of descent. 6.30
3.05　*Bray Creek* in big valley (sign). 6.22
3.08　Switchback to R and ascend steadily. 6.19
3.13　Top of rise. 6.14
3.22　Bottom of descent. 6.05
3.30　Top of rise; views open. 5.97
3.39　Descend. 5.88
3.41　Cross small wash in valley; ascend. 5.86
3.43　Switchback to L. 5.84
3.45　Top of rise; descend steadily to NNE. 5.82
3.48　Bottom of descent in semi-open area. 5.79
3.51　Bottom of descent; ascend steadily ENE; side-hill above steep valley. 5.76
3.67　Descend steadily. 5.60
3.68　*East Bray Creek* (often flowing). Parallel creek on other side. 5.59
3.73　Switchback to R; ascend steadily. 5.54
3.77　Top of rise; views (6,470'). 5.50
3.93　Bottom of descent. 5.34
4.00　Bottom of descent. 5.27
4.02　Top of rise; descend. 5.25
4.04　Cross small valley. 5.23
4.17　Top of rise. Descend into valley. 5.10
4.21　Sinkhole on R; sign "N Sycamore Creek". Descend bank. 5.06
4.23　Cross *North Sycamore Creek* (elevation 6,460'). 5.04
4.41　Landmark: go between cut ends of a log. 4.86
4.46　Bottom of descent, turn L. 4.81
4.50　Top of rise. 4.77
4.52　Top of rise. 4.75
4.68　Top of rise. Easy walking in semi-open forest. 4.59

4.84 Top of rise. 4.43
4.88 Switchback to L. 4.39
4.91 Switchback to R. Reach top of rise. Descend. 4.36
4.92 Cross dry creek. Ascend. 4.35
4.96 Top of rise. 4.31
5.03 Top of rise in low pass (6,230'). 4.24
5.07 Top of rise. 4.20
5.13 Views open to eastern Rim. 4.14
5.16 Switchback to R. 4.11
5.18 Cross creek valley. Side-hill out of it. 4.09
5.26 Top of rise. 4.01
5.39 Dip. 3.88
5.43 Top of rise. 3.84
5.48 Cross small valley. 3.79
5.51 Cross small dry creek. 3.76
5.54 Top of rise. 3.73
5.56 Cross small dip. 3.71
5.60 Top of rise, pass (6,020'). 3.67
5.71 Top of rise. 3.56
5.77 Cross *West Chase Creek* (sign). Ascend out of valley. 3.50
5.81 Top of rise. 3.46
5.89 [start of trenched section] 3.38
6.06 Cross through nice forest. 3.21
6.09 Cross small creek in area of red rocks. 3.18
6.15 Top of rise. Descend. 3.12
6.26 Cross small (usually) dry creek. Sign "West Chase Creek" is in error. 3.01
6.29 Top of rise. 2.98
6.34 Bottom of descent. 2.93
6.42 Top of rise in small pass. 2.85
6.56 Cross *East Chase Creek*. 2.71
6.57 Sign on tree: "Washington Park 1; Bray Creek 3". Ascend. 2.70
6.73 Cross red rocks in semi-open area. 2.54
6.75 Top of rise. 2.52
6.79 Switchback to R. Canyon below on L. 2.48
6.82 Switchback to L. 2.45
7.00 Top of rise. 2.27
7.03 Bottom of descent. 2.24
7.08 Top of rise. 2.19
7.22 Reach plateau (some views). 2.05
7.28 Landmark: double-trunked large alligator juniper tree. 1.99
7.30 Top of rise. 1.97
7.36 Switchback to L. [trenched, eroded section]..................................... 1.91
7.44 Cross creek. 1.83
7.49 Descend gradually through attractive area along side of creek. 1.78
7.63 Level area. 1.64
7.88 Ascend. Trail is rocky and goes up and down. 1.39
7.96 Turn R away from barbed-wire fence. 1.31
8.02 Switchback to L. 1.25
8.07 Switchback to R. 1.20
8.16 Switchback to L. Descend steadily. 1.11
8.18 Switchback to R. 1.09
8.23 Switchback to L. 1.04
8.27 Switchback to R and down. 1.00

8.29	Turn L, descend.	0.98
8.31	Cross road, then *Mail Creek* (6,040').	0.96
8.33	Turn R on alternate road, then L, ascending on trail.	0.94
8.40	Bottom of descent.	0.77
8.88	Attractive area through forest. Power line below on R.	0.39
9.00	**Junction:** cross power line service road.	0.27
9.05	Swing L.	0.22
9.07	Swing R at bottom of descent.	0.20
9.10	Top of rise.	0.17
9.14	Switchback to L, in small sag.	0.13
9.17	Bear L, on level.	0.10
9.21	**Junction:** trail of use on L.	0.06
9.22	**Important junction:** Col. Devin Trail [290] ascends to L, 2 miles to FR 300.	0.05
9.23	Corral on R.	0.04
9.25	**Junction:** main Highline Trail continues straight ahead where spur descends to TH parking.	0.02
9.27	Washington Park TH at end of FR 32A (elevation 6,250').	0.00

[31] Highline Trail WEST to EAST

Washington Park (FR 32A) to FR 289 (Tonto Creek)

Introduction. This is a *very long section* of trail between access points; it is 9.6 miles just between FR 144, a rough 4WD road, and the Tonto Fish Hatchery. For day hikers, a section can be done via the Myrtle Trail and Babe Haught Trails if 2 cars are used on the Rim Road [FR 300], or using a 4WD, accessing rough FR 144. The section that was burned in the 1990 and 2002 fires is subject to blowdowns which can slow travel considerably.

The Dude Fire. From east of Washington Park near Dude Creek all the way to east of FR 289, almost all the way to Horton Spring, the area below the Rim was burned. This will affect travel through the area for many years to come. The fire began from a lightning strike on June 25, 1990, during a period of drought, low humidity, and very high temperatures, and quickly became an inferno. At the time this was the largest fire in Arizona history. Why was this fire so much worse than others? The explanations include the weather conditions, the large accumulations of fuel due to the prevention of the spread of previous fires in an area in which they are natural, and little thinning of the forest (greater than ideal density). By the time the fire was contained 10 days later, over 24,000 acres had been burned, most of it in the Tonto National Forest, but some in the Coconino and Apache-Sitgreaves. Six lives were lost along with 36 million board feet of lumber, cattle, and wildlife. Over 1,100 people had to be evacuated. Since vegetation holding topsoil was burned, subsequent rains washed much of it away. Salvage logging, re-seeding, tree planting, fencing to prevent cattle from eating the sprouting new vegation are some of the rehabilitation steps that have been taken.* The fire's aftermath can be expected to continue to present problems in Highline Trail and side-trail maintenance. (In June of 2002 the even worse Rodeo-Chediski Fire raged out of control near the Rim and forced the evacuation of many more people. Other fires were burning near Payson in 2004.)

Maps. *Our Maps 7-12 (Highline 7 to Highline 12).* The USGS 1:24,000 Kehl Ridge and Dane Canyon quadrangles (1972) cover part of the trail route. On the Dane Canyon map much of the route is still correct. On Kehl Ridge, the trail location descending to the East Verde River is changed.

Access. *At the western end* from Washington Park Trailhead at the end of FR 32A, 0.5 mile off FR 32, 3.3 miles from the Control Road [FR 64]. *At the eastern end*, from FR 289 at the Hatchery Trailhead, 4.8 miles north of SR 260. *Note that in wet weather the lower end of FR 32A may be muddy and impassable for 2WD vehicles.*

General Description. From the Washington Park Trailhead, the Highline Trail fords the East Verde River and ascends the flank of the ridge for 0.25 mile to meet the Pump Station Trail [296] and continues its climb to 0.5 mile. It then side-hills the flank of the Rim up and down, crossing Dude Creek at 2.5

---

*We wish to acknowledge the assistance of the Forest Service's publication *The Story of Dude Fire*, published 5/91.

miles, where the 1990 Dude Fire area is entered. There is then a gradual 300' ascent (crossing Dry Dude Creek on the way) to a pass on a small ridge, whereupon the trail makes a long descent through a valley for another 300' (with much brush and down trees). Fuller Creek is crossed at 4.5 miles. The trail then ascends to almost 6,800', drops to cross Bonita Creek at 5.5 miles, then descends 200' in elevation down its valley before an ascent of 200' to meet the end of FR 144 at 6.5 miles. The trail continues up and down to a junction with the Myrtle Trail [30] at 8.4 miles. At 9.6 miles it crosses Ellison Creek, making a long descent down its valley. A gradual ascent of 600' to cross Roberts Mesa leads to FR 289C at 15.5 miles near the Zane Grey Cabin site. Another 0.6 mile of scenic descent brings one to FR 289 at Tonto Creek at 16.1 miles. Total elevation gain is 1,200' to FR 144 and 1,200' to Tonto Creek, a total of about 2,400'.

The Tonto Creek Hatchery is worth a visit. It was built on the old Babe Haught homestead in 1935 by the Works Progress Administration [WPA]. It was rebuilt after a disastrous flood in 1970, and completely rebuilt in 1989 along with a visitor center and self-guided tour. 250 thousand catchable trout are produced annually.[1]

Famous Western novelist (56 in all) Zane Grey's cabin[2] was burned in the Dude Fire, but efforts of the Zane Grey Cabin Foundation will lead to a rebuilding of a replica at the site of the Rim Country Museum in Payson.

Cautions. Crossing the East Verde River can be difficult after wet weather. It may need to be waded. Several other creeks, especially Bonita and Dude, can also be difficult. The blowdowns that inevitably occur annually after a major fire will slow down travelers, and there is much up and down travel.

Read Down ↓	Detailed Trail Description	Read Up ↑
0.00	From the parking area at Washington Park [FR 32A], head N at sign, uphill. In 85' join Highline Trail [measured from this point]; go R (E) on it (6,080').	16.09
0.04	**Junction:** at vehicleway, turn L toward river (R back to TH in 140').	16.05
0.07	Turn R, descend to river bank. Cross *East Verde River*.	16.02
0.08	Far side of river. Ascend to L, then R.	16.01
0.15	Sag.	15.94
0.17	Top of rise.	15.92
0.23	**Junction:** trail [296], Pump Station Trail, heads R, 0.9 mi down to pump station, requiring crossing of E Verde River. Bear L, ascending. [GPS 0486185/3809580]	15.86
0.26	Little sag.	15.83
0.35	Sag.	15.74
0.37	Switchback to L and ascend.	15.72
0.48	Ease grade of ascent.	15.61
0.51	**Junction:** well-worn NDT on R. No sign. Cairn marks wrong trail. Continue straight ahead. [GPS 0486515/3809365] Top of rise on ridge.	15.58
0.60	Top of rise.	15.49
0.64	Cross small valley.	15.45

---

[1]*Tonto Creek Hatchery.* Brochure [undated] produced by Arizona Game & Fish Dept., 2221 W. Greenway Rd., Phoenix 85023.
[2]It was on the National Register of Historic Places.

0.66	Sag.	15.43
0.68	Turn L.	15.41
0.79	Beautiful walk thru forest.	15.30
0.84	Top of rise.	15.25
0.88	Top of rise.	15.21
0.93	Sag.	15.16
0.94	Switchback to L.	15.15
0.97	Switchback to R.	15.12
1.03	Start descent.	15.06
1.07	Top of rise. Viewpoint to W. [GPS 0486905/3808900]	15.02
1.22	Swing to R, then down to L.	14.87
1.24	Cross creek; ascend.	14.85
1.26	Switchback to R.	14.83
1.34	Top of rise.	14.75
1.42	Top of rise.	14.67
1.45	Junction: alternate trail angles to L. Keep R. In 25' at bottom of descent, turn L. [GPS 0487130/3808420]	14.64
1.47	Sag.	14.62
1.58	Sag.	14.51
1.59	Switchback to L.	14.50
1.60	Switchback to R.	14.49
1.64	Cross small creek in sag.	14.45
1.66	Turn L.	14.43
1.74	Top of rise.	14.35
1.88	Important Junction: vehicleway sharp R; go L on vehicleway on level.	14.21
2.05	Top of rise (6,270').	14.04
2.09	Dip.	14.00
2.10	Top of rise.	13.99
2.16	Cross over rocks.	13.93
2.19	Cross flat rocks.	13.90
2.23	Dip.	13.86
2.40	Pass. Vehicleway ends, trail starts. [GPS 0488090/3807750]	13.69
2.43	Switchback down to R.	13.66
2.46	Turn R, ease descent, then parallel Dude Creek. [GPS 0488175/3807810]	13.63
2.52	Drop steeply down bank.	13.57
2.54	Cross *Dude Creek*. [GPS 0488060/3800690]	13.55
2.56	Switchback up to L.	13.53
2.74	Top of rise.	13.35
3.03	Bear L.	13.06
3.18	Junction: go L on vehicleway. [GPS 0488895/3807480]	12.91
3.21	Top of rise. Go thru gate in barbed-wire fence, then turn R & then L. [GPS 0480855/3800400]	12.88
3.42	Cross *Dry Dude Creek* (not dry!). [GPS 0489145/3807325]	12.67
3.44	Switchback to L.	12.65
3.52	Turn L.	12.57
3.74	Top of rise.	12.35
3.79	Top of ridge (6,650'). [GPS 0489340/3807190]	12.30
3.85	Switchback to R, descend.	12.24
4.16	Cross to other side of valley	11.93
4.22	Go around toe of minor ridge.	11.87
4.24	Junction: game trail on L; keep R. [GPS 0489220/3806730]	11.85
4.33	Top of rise.	11.76
4.40	Bottom of descent.	11.69

4.43	Switchback to L.	11.66
4.51	Top of rise.	11.58
4.54	Cross *Fuller Creek* [often dry]. [GPS 0489475/3806420]	11.55
4.57	Top of rise.	11.52
4.67	Top of rise.	11.42
4.75	Top of rise.	11.34
4.85	Top of rise.	11.24
4.91	Turn L.	11.18
4.94	Bottom of descent.	11.15
4.95	Top of rise.	11.14
4.98	Bottom of descent.	11.11
4.99	Switchback to L.	11.10
5.07	**Junction (4-way):** cross old vehicleway. [GPS 0480000/3806180]	11.02
5.10	Top of rise.	10.99
5.11	Turn L.	10.98
5.16	Turn L.	10.93
5.34	Go R.	10.75
5.36	Go thru hiker's gate in barbed-wire fence. [GPS 0480395/3806250]	10.73
5.38	Pass (6,550').	10.71
5.41	**Junction:** NDT trail angles L. [GPS 0480495/3806230]	10.68
5.53	*Bonita Creek.* [GPS 0480485/3800265]	10.56
5.67	Top of rise.	10.42
5.72	Top of rise.	10.37
5.75	Top of rise.	10.34
5.82	Top of rise.	10.27

10.78 Go thru gate. 5.31
10.96 Cross creek. 5.13
11.18 Steep pitch up. 4.91
11.27 **Junction:** sharp R is stock trail. (On return, keep R here.) 4.82
11.38 Bottom of descent. 4.71
11.52 Start descent into valley. 4.57
11.60 Bottom of descent; ascend along wash. 4.49
11.62 Top of rise. 4.47
11.64 Cross wash. 4.45
11.69 Steep pitch up. 4.40
11.72 Cross open rocks. 4.37
11.74 Turn R, ascend. In 50', turn L. 4.35
11.90 Top of rise. 4.19
12.12 Start descent into valley. 3.97
12.20 Cross wash in canyon. 3.89
12.28 Top of rise. 3.81
12.40 Top of ridge with fine views. 3.69
12.43 Hiker's gate. 3.66
12.46 Switchback to L. 3.63
12.54 Bottom of descent. 3.55
12.56 Top of rise. 3.53
12.64 Cross creek. 3.45
12.78 Top of rise. 3.31
12.93 Cross bare hillside. 3.16
12.99 **Junction (5-way):** trail of use on L; vehicleway on R & sharp L. 3.10
13.15 Cross seep on rocks. 2.94
13.38 Top of rise on open rock. Canyon below on R. 2.71
14.04 Cross creek. 2.05
14.05 Turn L. 2.04
14.10 Bottom of descent; cross wash. 1.99
14.13 Turn L. 1.96
14.14 Switchback to R [blow-down area]. 1.95
14.20 Top of rise. 1.89
14.29 Turn L. 1.70
14.62 Cross small wash. 1.47
14.83 Electrified fence (signs) on R. 1.26
15.00 Switchback to L. 1.09
15.10 Cross creek. 0.99
15.12 Electric fence on R; switchback to R. 0.97
15.33 Hiker's gate. 0.76
15.38 Switchback R. 0.71
15.50 **Important junction:** cross FR 289C at gate. Zane Grey estates to L. 0.59
15.61 Leave vehicleway; cross open rocks. 0.48
15.65 Top of rise; descend. 0.44
15.68 Cliff area. 0.41
15.70 Cross open rocks. 0.39
15.89 Top of rise. 0.20
15.90 Cross rocky small wash. 0.15
15.98 Switchback down to L. 0.11
16.05 Top of rise. 0.04
16.08 Switchback R. 0.01
16.09 Tonto Creek Road [FR 289] parking area below Fish Hatchery (6,120'). 0.00

[31] Highline Trail WEST to EAST

FR 289 (Tonto Creek) to FR 284 (Christopher Creek/See Canyon)

Introduction. This is a long section, 10.75 miles, broken for most hikers by a car shuttle or circuits with shuttles from the Derrick Trail [33] or Horton Creek Trail [285]. This is a strenuous hike as a through trip, despite the lack of major ascents.

Maps. *Our Maps 12-14 (Highline 12 to Highline 14).* The USGS 1:24,000 Promontory Butte and Knoll Lake quadrangles (1973) cover part of the trail, but not on the correct current location.

Access. *At the western end,* from Tonto Fish Hatchery. *At the eastern end,* from See Canyon Road (FR 284), 1.6 miles north of SR 260.

General Description. Leaving the trailhead, Tonto Creek is crossed and a short ascent over a shoulder leads to Dick Williams Creek, then to a fine viewpoint at 1.75 miles. An easy ascent leads to the junction with the Horton Creek Trail [285] at 3.4 miles. Horton Springs Trail [292] and the Springs are passed. A brief rise over a ridge brings one to the East Fork of Horton Creek at 4 miles. There is then a steady 400' ascent out of that valley to the south, then along the flank of Promontory Butte to the Derrick Trail [33] at 6.4 miles. Here the direction changes abruptly to the east and north. A high point is reached at 7.3 miles, and a good viewpoint at 8.3 miles. The remainder of the trail goes up and down, then descends steadily for the last half mile to See Canyon at 10.75 miles. Total elevation gain is 1,820'.

Read Down ↓	Detailed Trail Description	Read Up ↑
0.00	From FR 289 below the Tonto Fish Hatchery, head E. Elevation 6,140'.	
	Switchback down to L in 75'.	10.75
0.04	Switchback down to R.	10.71
0.06	**Junction:** go R.	10.69
0.11	**Junction:** go L, to creek (6,090').	10.64
0.13	Cross Tonto Creek, bear R, then ascend steadily to SE on rocky trail.	10.62
0.27	**Junction:** avoid trail straight ahead; keep R.	10.48
0.28	Top of rise. Descend gradually to E.	10.47
0.31	Cross creek, ascend.	10.44
0.35	Switchback R, to L in 55'.	10.40
0.45	Switchback R.	10.30
0.52	Switchback L into open, rocky area.	10.23
0.56	Ease, then ascend to E, views open.	10.19
0.66	Level off (6,390').	10.09
0.77	**Junction:** avoid old trail; switchback to L, descending to SE.	9.98
0.85	**Junction:** avoid trail straight ahead; switchback to L.	9.90
0.86	Switchback R along Dick Williams Creek.	9.99
0.88	Cross *Dick Williams Creek.*	9.87
0.98	Top of rise.	9.77
1.18	Bottom of descent.	9.57
1.35	Top of rise.	9.40
1.36	Cross small creek, ascend steadily R (S), then SSE.	9.39

4.91	Top of rise in draw.	5.84
4.95	Emerge from draw.	5.80
5.09	**Junction:** old vehicleway (blocked) on R.	5.66
5.13	Bottom of descent.	5.62
5.36	Top of rise.	5.39
5.46	Bottom of descent with rocky spires above.	5.29
5.51	Pass.	5.24
5.56	Bottom of descent; cross valley bottom, ascend.	5.19
5.60	Top of rise.	5.15
5.62	Sign "Horton Spring 2".	5.13
5.66	**Important junction:** site of former Promontory Trail [278].	5.09
5.75	Turn R (S).	5.00
5.90	Turn L.	4.85
6.01	**Junction:** spur R leads down to viewpoint on ledge.	4.74
6.05	Top of rise.	4.70
6.12	Go along top of sandstone formation, with views.	4.63
6.16	Top of rise.	4.59
6.30	Cross rock.	4.45
6.38	**Junction:** Derrick Trail [33] (6,560'). *This location is 0.25 mi SW of the location shown on the topo map.*	4.37

6.38	Leave Derrick Trail junction, heading NE.	4.37
6.39	Go thru barbed-wire fence (open).	4.36
6.70	Cross draw.	4.05
6.79	Bottom of descent.	3.96
6.82	Turn L.	3.93
6.89	Top of rise.	3.86
6.94	Turn R.	3.81
6.96	Turn L.	3.79
6.98	Bottom of descent.	3.77
7.00	Cross draw and wash.	3.75
7.13	Switchback to L. Side-hill beside deep valley, with views.	3.62
7.14	Switchback to R.	3.61
7.27	Top of rise, pass (6,740').	3.48
7.38	Cross draw...	3.37
7.46	Bottom of descent.	3.29
7.57	Bottom of descent.	3.18
7.63	**Junction:** viewpoint uphill 100' to R (6,700').	3.12
7.66	Bottom of descent.	3.09
7.73	Top of rise. Descend steadily.	3.02
7.75	Bottom of descent.	3.00
7.78	Cross wash in draw.	2.97
7.82	Top of rise.	2.93
7.84	Top of rise.	2.91
7.87	Top of rise.	2.88
7.89	Top of rise. Turn R (S).	2.86
7.98	Top of rise.	2.77
8.02	Top of rise.	2.73
8.09	Cross wash in small draw.	2.66
8.32	Spectacular viewpoint off to R.	2.43
8.36	Cross wash.	2.39
8.39	Views to S.	2.36
8.43	Top of rise.	2.32
8.45	Top of rise. Descend steep grade.	2.30
8.49	Cross wash in draw.	2.26
8.53	Switchback to L.	2.22
8.58	Keep L.	2.17
8.63	Bottom of descent.	2.12
8.65	**Junction:** viewpoint 100' to R on rock formations.	2.10
8.73	Viewpoint to S.	2.02
8.76	Cross wash.	1.99
8.79	Top of rise.	1.96
8.93	**Junction:** keep R; old route (blocked) on L.	1.82
8.95	Turn L.	1.80
9.00	**Junction:** ignore old vehicleway on L.	1.75
9.01	Top of rise.	1.74
9.04	Cross small creek in draw.	1.71
9.16	Level in nice area.	1.59
9.32	Cross wash.	1.43
9.36	Top of rise.	1.39
9.44	Cross wash in sag.	1.31
9.46	Top of rise.	1.29
9.55	Cross creek in draw.	1.20
9.71	Large flat area (6,500').	1.04

9.85	Swing L.	0.90
9.91	Open flat area. Old vehicleway (blocked) descends to E here.	0.84
10.02	Top of rise.	0.73
10.04	Cross moderate wash.	0.71
10.07	Top of rise.	0.68
10.10	Top of rise (6,460').	0.65
10.32	Turn L in attractive area.	0.43
10.34	Top of rise (6,450').	0.41
10.42	Eroded section.	0.33
10.62	Bear L.	0.13
10.66	Swing R.	0.09
10.68	Switchback to L.	0.07
10.69	Switchback to R.	0.06
10.75	Christopher Creek/See Canyon Road [FR 284] 0.1 mi S of trailhead parking area (6,160').	0.00

[31] Highline Trail WEST to EAST

See Canyon/Christopher Creek [FR 284] to Two-Sixty Trailhead

Introduction. This first section of the Highline Trail west of 260 Trailhead makes for good walking or riding. Using a 2-vehicle shuttle, this makes a good but fairly easy day's walk. A long circuit trip can be taken using the Military Sinkhole Trail [179], Highline Trail, Drew Trail [291] and FR 9350 and 300 back to the Military Sinkhole Trail.

Maps. *Our Maps 15-17 (Highline 15: See4 Canyon, Highline 16: Drew Trail, and Highline 17: 260 Trailhead).* The USGS 1:24,000 Woods Canyon (Provisional Edition, 1990) and Promontory Butte (1973) quadrangles cover the approach and the former shows the trail, although the actual location deviates somewhat from what is shown.

Access. *At the western end,* from FR 284, 1.6 miles north of Sr 260, and 0.1 mile south of the trailhead parking area. *At the eastern end,* from Two-Sixty Trailhead just off SR 260, 24 miles east of Payson [will be shorter when the new highway alignment is completed].

General Description. This last trail section crosses FR 284 0.1 mile south of See Canyon Trailhead, then crosses Christopher Creek, meets the See Canyon Trail [184] and ascends gradually out of the valley along the flank of the Rim, passing many creeks and a good viewpoint to 2.2 miles where the Drew Trail [291] ascends steeply up to the Rim and FR 300. At 4.25 miles there is a good viewpoinmt and lunch spot. Crossing several creeks and small valleys, the trail finally reaches the 260 Trailhead at 6.4 miles. *Please note that in or after wet weather it may be difficult to cross Christopher Creek.* Total ascent is 700', descent is 100'.

Read Down ↓	Detailed Trail Description	Read Up ↑
0.00	From FR 284 (6,160') TH parking is 0.1 mi N.	6.36
0.03	**Junction:** vehicleway goes R.	6.33
0.04	**Junction:** trail of use from R.	6.32
0.08	**Junction:** trail on L to parking area.	6.28
0.10	**Junction:** trail on W side.	6.26
0.11	Cross *Christopher Creek* (one of 2 crossing places). Ascend.	6.25
0.13	Ease ascent. Camping area.	6.23
0.14	**Junction:** trail joins from L.	6.20
0.17	**Junction:** trail on L is See Canyon [184]. Sign says "Rim Road 2_, See Spring Spring _". [Actual distances are 3.55 and 0.68 mi, respectively.]	6.19
0.23	Bottom of valley (6,140').	6.13
0.26	**Junction:** alternate trail.	6.10
0.33	Top of rise.	6.03
0.35	Cross creek (6,190').	6.01
0.38	Switchback to L at barbed-wire fence.	5.98
0.41	Switchback to R.	5.95
0.46	Top of rise.	5.90
0.53	Top of rise (6,240').	5.83
0.58	Cross creek.	5.78

0.65	Switchbacks (4).	5.71
0.66	Bottom of descent.	5.70
0.87	Top of rise.	5.49
0.97	Top of rise.	5.39
0.98	Bottom of descent.	5.38
1.01	Bottom of descent in creek valley.	5.35
1.06	Top of rise (6,250').	5.30
1.10	Top of rise.	5.25
1.12	Cross major creek where it turns to S.	5.24
1.39	Bottom of descent.	4.97
1.83	Cross creek.	4.53
1.90	Switchback to R.	4.46
1.98	Switchback to L at small creek.	4.38
2.08	Switchback to R.	4.28
2.12	Switchback to L.	4.24
2.24	**Important junction:** Drew Trail [291] L to Rim in 1.1 mi; elevation here 6,790'.	4.12
2.93	Landmark: go between cut tree ends.	3.43
3.16	Flat, semi-open area with views (6,760').	3.20
3.25	Top of rise.	3.15
3.26	Cross creek in valley.	3.14
3.37	Top of rise (6,770').	3.03
3.41	Top of rise.	2.99
3.50	Top of rise.	2.90
3.57	Bottom of descent.	2.83
3.65	Top of rise.	2.71
3.75	Cross small creek.	2.61
3.83	Top of rise.	2.53
3.99	Cross small creek in valley.	2.37
4.10	Top of rise.	2.26
4.23	Viewpoint along the Rim.	2.13
4.25	Top of subsidiary spur with good views (6,720'); good lunch spot.	2.11
4.32	Top of rise.	2.04
4.41	Top of rise on semi-open ridge.	1.95
4.52	Top of rise.	1.84
4.55	Cross creek.	1.81
4.65	Top of rise.	1.71
4.68	Cross several small drainages.	1.68
4.73	Top of rise.	1.63
4.90	Cross moderate creek.	1.46
4.98	Top of rise.	1.38
5.01	Cross 2 small creeks.	1.35
5.10	Top of rise.	1.26
5.27	Cross major creek (6,640').	1.09
5.51	Top of rise.	0.85
5.64	Cross creek.	0.72
5.70	Cross creek.	0.66
6.06	Top of rise.	0.30
6.18	Cross small creek on smooth rocks.	0.18
6.36	**Junction:** Two-Sixty Trailhead (6,660'). *This trail ends.*	0.00

SR 260 is just down the spur road to the right. The Military Sinkhole Trail [179] continues ahead to reach FR 300 on the Rim in 2.35 miles.

The Highline Trail

Trail Descriptions

Direction:

EAST to WEST

[31] **Highline Trail** EAST to WEST

Two-Sixty Trailhead to See Canyon/Christopher Creek [FR 284]

Introduction. This first section of the Highline Trail west of 260 Trailhead makes for good walking or riding. Using a 2-vehicle shuttle, this makes a good but fairly easy day's walk. A long circuit trip can be taken using the Military Sinkhole Trail [179], Highline Trail, Drew Trail [291] and FR 9350 and 300 back to the Military Sinkhole Trail.

Maps. *Our Maps 15-17 (Highline 15: See Canyon, Highline 16: Drew Trail, and Highline 17: 260 Trailhead).* The USGS 1:24,000 Woods Canyon (Provisional Edition, 1990) and Promontory Butte (1973) quadrangles cover the approach and the former shows the trail, although the actual location deviates somewhat from what is shown.

Access. *At the eastern end,* from Two-Sixty Trailhead just off SR 260, 24 miles east of Payson [will be shorter when the new highway alignment is completed]. *At the western end,* from FR 284, 1.6 miles north of SR 260, and 0.1 mile south of trailhead parking area.

General Description. This trail section, the first west of 260 Trailhead, commences slabbing the side of the Rim, passing many creeks and a good viewpoint and lunch spot at 2.1 miles, to 4.1 miles, where the Drew Trail [291] leads steeply 1.1 miles up to the Rim and FR 300. This section requires considerable up-and-down travel. From the junction, the trail descends steadily down a branch of Christopher Creek for almost 500' in elevation at 5.25 miles, then heads west and north around a shoulder to cross another creek at 6 miles. After a short rise it descends gradually into See Canyon and meets the See Canyon Trail [184] at 6.2 miles, crosses Christopher Creek at 6.25 miles, then angles southwest to cross FR 284 0.1 mile south of the See Canyon trailhead. *Please note that in or after wet weather it may be difficult to cross Christopher Creek.* Total ascent is 100', descent is 700'.

Read Down ↓	Detailed Trail Description	Read Up ↑
0.00	From the Two-Sixty Trailhead (6,660') this trail heads west.	6.36
0.18	Cross small creek on smooth rocks.	6.18
0.30	Top of rise.	6.06
0.66	Cross creek, follow it up, ascending.	5.70
0.72	Cross creek.	5.64
0.85	Top of rise.	5.51
1.09	Cross major creek (6,640'). Easy walking.	5.27
1.26	Top of rise.	5.10
1.35	Cross small creek, then another.	5.01
1.38	Top of rise.	4.98
1.46	Cross moderate creek; ascend.	4.90
1.63	Top of rise.	4.73
1.68	Cross several small drainages.	4.68
1.81	Cross creek.	4.55
1.84	Top of rise; head W on level trail.	4.52
1.95	Top of rise on semi-open ridge.	4.41

2.11	Top of subsidiary spur with good views (6,720'); good lunch spot.	4.25
2.13	Viewpoint along the Rim.	4.23
2.26	Top of rise.	4.10
2.37	Cross small creek in valley.	3.99
2.53	Top of rise.	3.83
2.61	Cross small creek; ascend steadily.	3.75
2.64	Top of rise.	3.72
2.83	Bottom of descent.	3.57
2.90	Top of rise.	3.50
2.99	Top of rise.	3.41
3.03	Top of rise (6,770'); side-hill down above deep valley.	3.37
3.14	Cross creek in valley.	3.26
3.15	Top of rise.	3.25
3.20	Flat, semi-open area with views (6,760').	3.16
3.43	Landmark: go between cut tree ends.	2.93
4.12	**Junction:** Drew Trail [291] R to Rim in 1.1 mi; elevation 6,790'. Continue descending SSW, taking trail to L. Start is not obvious, but there is a cairn. Use care.	2.24
4.24	Switchback to R (alternate trail close by).	2.12
4.28	Switchback to L.	2.08
4.38	Switchback to L at small creek. Head W.	1.98
4.46	Switchback to L, then to R in 35'.	1.90
4.53	Cross creek, ascend gradually away from it.	1.83
4.63	Descend steadily.	1.73
4.95	Side-hill above creek, then descend.	1.41
5.24	Cross major creek where it turns to S.	1.12
5.25	Top of rise. Head S.	1.10
5.30	Top of rise (6,250').	1.06
5.35	Bottom of descent. Cross creek valley.	1.01
5.39	Top of rise.	0.97
5.70	Bottom of descent.	0.66
5.71	Switchback to L and to R, then to L in 65', and to R in 80'.	0.65
5.78	Cross creek.	0.58
5.83	Top of rise (6,240'). Head SSW.	0.53
5.90	Top of rise. Descend steadily to W.	0.46
5.95	Switchback to L, to S.	0.41
5.98	Switchback to R at barbed-wire fence.	0.38
6.01	Cross creek from R (6,190').	0.35
6.03	Top of rise.	0.33
6.10	**Junction:** other trail on R is wider (6,150').	0.26
6.13	Bottom of valley (6,140').	0.23
6.19	**Junction:** trail on R is See Canyon [184]. Sign says "Rim Road 21/2, See Spring 1/2.". [Actual distances are 3.55 and 0.68 mi respectively.]	0.17
6.20	**Junction:** trail joins from R (from [184]).	0.16
6.23	Camping area. Descend steeply to creek.	0.13
6.25	Cross *Christopher Creek* (one of 2 crossing places).	0.11
6.26	**Junction:** trail on W side. Ascend.	0.10
6.28	**Junction:** trail on R to parking area. Continue to S.	0.08
6.32	**Junction:** keep L.	0.04
6.33	**Junction:** vehicleway goes L.	0.03
6.36	**Junction:** FR 284 in See Canyon (6,160'). TH parking is 0.1 mi N on road. Highline Trail continues W across road.	0.00

[31] Highline Trail EAST to WEST

FR 284 (Christopher Creek/See Canyon) to FR 289 (Tonto Creek)

Introduction. This is a long section, 10.75 miles, broken for most hikers by a car shuttle or circuits with shuttles from the Derrick Trail [33] or Horton Creek Trail [285]. As a through trip, this is a strenuous hike with fine views, despite the lack of major ascents.

Maps. *Our Maps 12-15 (Highline 12 to Highline 15).* The USGS 1:24,000 Promontory Butte quadrangle (1973, airphotos 1965) covers some of the trail, but part of it is in a changed location.

Access. *At the eastern end,* from See Canyon Road (FR 284), 1.6 miles north of SR 260. *At the western end,* from FR 289 just south of the Fish Hatchery.

General Description. This trail ascends the face of the Rim (Promontory Butte) for 350', then side-hills along, crossing several creeks, passing a viewpoint at 2.1 miles and very fine ones at 2.4 and 3.1 miles, to the Derrick trail at 4.4 miles. The highest point reached is 6,740'. Beyond, another 3 miles of ups and downs brings one to the East Fork of Horton Creek and then another rise and descent to Horton Springs, and the Horton Springs [292] and Horton Creek [285] Trails at 7.3 miles. Continuing, there are some viewpoints and Dick Williams Creek is crossed at 9.9 miles. After a descent, Tonto Creek is crossed at 10.6 miles and finally FR 289 is reached at 10.75 miles. Total elevation gain is about 1,250'.

Read Down ↓	Detailed Trail Description	Read Up ↑
0.00	From the Christopher Creek/See Canyon Road [FR 284] 0.1 mi S of the trailhead parking area (6,160'), head NW, uphill.	10.75
0.06	Switchback to L.	10.69
0.07	Switchback to R, heading W.	10.68
0.09	Swing L.	10.66
0.13	Bear R (SW), then to W.	10.62
0.33	Eroded section.	10.42
0.41	Top of rise (6,450').	10.34
0.43	Turn R (NW), then level off. Attractive area.	10.32
0.65	Top of rise (6,460'). Descend gradually, bear R (W).	10.10
0.68	Descend steadily.	10.07
0.71	Cross moderate wash. Ascend to L.	10.04
0.73	Top of rise. Head S, level.	10.02
0.84	Open flat area (old vehicleway, blocked, descends to E here).	9.91
0.90	Swing R (WNW) on level.	9.85
1.04	Large flat area (6,500'). Descend gradually W.	9.71
1.10	Ascend steadily WSW.	9.65
1.14	Descend steadily to WNW.	9.61
1.20	Cross creek in draw.	9.55
1.29	Top of rise.	9.46
1.31	Cross wash in sag.	9.44
1.39	Top of rise.	9.36

1.43	Cross wash.	9.32
1.59	Level in nice area.	9.16
1.71	Cross small creek in draw, ascending to W.	9.04
1.74	Top of rise.	9.01
1.75	**Junction:** old vehicleway on R. Trail becomes narrower, brushier.	9.00
1.80	Turn R (N).	8.95
1.82	**Junction:** turn L where old route (blocked) goes R.	8.93
1.96	Top of rise.	8.79
1.99	Cross wash. Trail widens; easy walking.	8.76
2.02	Viewpoint to S.	8.73
2.10	Top of rise. In 45' is **junction:** viewpoint 100' to L on rock formations. Descend steadily to W, then to SW.	8.65
2.12	Bottom of descent.	8.63
2.17	Keep R (trail ahead blocked; trail of use to spur with some views). Descend.	8.58
2.20	Descend steadily, side-hilling to SW.	8.55
2.22	Switchback to R (N).	8.53
2.26	Cross wash in draw, then side-hill steeply up.	8.49
2.30	Top of rise. Go up & down.	8.45
2.32	Top of rise. Descend steadily.	8.43
2.36	Views to S. Ascend gradually.	8.39
2.39	Cross wash. Attractive area, above rocks.	8.36
2.43	Spectacular viewpoint off to L.	8.32
2.66	Cross wash in small draw; head into forest, to NW.	8.09
2.73	Top of rise. Cross wash.	8.02
2.77	Top of rise. Descend into valley.	7.98

2.86   Top of rise; turn L (W). 7.89
2.88   Start ascent to NW on trenched trail. 7.87
2.91   Top of rise. 7.84
2.93   Start descending to NW. 7.82
2.97   Cross wash in draw; descend to S. 7.78
3.00   Start steady ascent. 7.75
3.02   Top of rise. Level briefly, then descend to S and SW. 7.73
3.09   Bottom of descent. Bear R, ascend rocky trail. 7.66
3.12   **Junction:** viewpoint uphill 100' to L (6,700'). Descend rocky trail to W. 7.63
3.18   Bottom of descent. 7.57
3.20   Start steady descent. 7.55
3.29   Bottom of descent; views. 7.46
3.37   Cross draw; start steady, rocky ascent. 7.38
3.48   Top of rise, pass (6,740'). Descend steadily to W. 7.27
3.61   Switchback to L; descend to S. 7.14
3.62   Switchback to R. Side-hill beside deep valley with views. 7.13
3.75   Cross draw and wash. 7.00
3.77   Bottom of descent. 6.98
3.79   Turn R, ascend steadily. 6.96
3.81   Turn L. 6.94
3.86   Top of rise. 6.89
3.93   Turn R (NNW). 6.82
3.96   Bottom of descent; in 100' top a rise. 6.79
4.05   Cross draw. 6.70
4.36   Go thru barbed-wire fence (open). 6.39
4.37   **Junction:** Derrick Trail [33] on L to Upper Tonto Campground in 2.20 mi.
       Highline Trail goes sharp R here, uphill (6,520').
       This location is 0.25 mi SW of the location shown on the topo map. 6.38

4.37   Leave junction with Derrick Trail [33]. 6.38
4.45   Cross rocks. 6.30
4.59   Top of rise. 6.16
4.63   Go along top of sandstone formations with views to S. 6.12
4.70   Top of rise. 6.05
4.74   **Junction:** spur L leads down to viewpoint on ledge. 6.01
4.85   Turn R. 5.90
5.00   Turn L (N), ascending gradually. 5.75
5.09   **Important junction:** site of Promontory Trail [278] on R. [This steep trail has
       a dangerous slump and the upper trailhead is difficult to find, so it has been
       deleted and is omitted from this guide.] 5.66
5.13   Sign "Horton Spring 2". 5.62
5.15   Start descending toward canyon. 5.60
5.19   Bottom of descent. Cross valley bottom. 5.56
5.24   Pass. 5.51
5.29   Bottom of descent. Cross above rocks, with rocky spires above. 5.46
5.39   Top of rise. 5.36
5.62   Bottom of descent. 5.13
5.66   **Junction:** old vehicleway (blocked) on L. 5.09
5.80   Go into draw, heading E. 4.95
5.84   Top of rise in draw. 4.91
5.87   Switchback to R, then to L in 100'. 4.88
5.90   Ascend across outwash valley with rocky ridges, to W. 4.85

5.96	Switchback to R, steeply up hogback, then to L in 90', then to R in 35' more.	4.79
6.00	Top of rise.	4.75
6.02	Cross gully, ascend L.	4.73
6.09	Switchback to R, then to L in 45'.	4.66
6.11	Top of rise.	4.64
6.32	Valley of Horton Creek in view ahead.	4.43
6.41	Switchback to R and descend to N.	4.34
6.62	Start steep descent.	4.13
6.64	Switchback to L, then to R in 165'.	4.11
6.79	Cross creek (East Fork, Horton Creek).	3.96
6.96	Acend steeply to L (N).	3.79
7.13	Top of rise.	3.62
7.16	**Junction:** at top of ridge, to viewpoint.	3.59
7.21	Switchback to R.	3.54
7.30	Cross outlet of Horton Spring.	3.45
7.31	**Junction:** Horton Springs Trail [292] ascends hillside on R [not signed in 2003].	3.44
7.34	**Junction:** Horton Creek Trail [285] to L (6,640') to Horton CG.	3.41

7.34	Leave **junction** with Horton Creek Trail [285] to L, heading W, paralleling that trail (old vehicleway) briefly and ascending.	3.41
7.43	Top of rise (6,680').	3.32
7.62	Top of rise.	3.13
7.66	Top of rise (6,600').	3.09
7.88	Top of rise.	2.93
7.85	Top of rise.	2.90
7.89	Cross creek.	2.86
7.90	Top of rise.	2.85
8.08	Switchback to L.	2.67
8.09	Top of rise; backward view into valley.	2.66
8.13	Top of rise (6,600').	2.62
8.20	Cross moderate creek.	2.55
8.21	Top of rise (6,550').	2.54
8.33	Cross side-creek.	2.42
8.34	**Junction:** go R (not straight).	2.41
8.44	Top of rise. Attractive area.	2.31
8.47	Top of rise.	2.28
8.55	Top of rise.	2.20
8.66	Top of rise.	2.09
8.70	Cross creek in draw.	2.05
8.73	**Junction:** go L	2.02
8.77	**Junction:** join power line service road coming from R.	1.98
8.78	Bottom of descent. Cross power line.	1.97
8.99	Switchback down to R. **Junction:** knob to S (viewpoint) is 405' away.	1.76
9.02	Switchback to L (6,480').	1.73
9.05	Top of rise.	1.70
9.09	Switchback to R, then to L in 40'.	1.66
9.13	**Junction:** alternate trail; keep R.	1.62
9.19	Switchback down to R.	1.56
9.25	**Junction:** avoid trail of use sharp R.	1.50
9.34	Turn R.	1.41
9.39	Cross small creek.	1.36
9.40	Top of rise.	1.35

9.57	Bottom of descent.	1.18
9.77	Top of rise.	0.98
9.87	Cross *Dick Williams Creek* (6,260'). Ascend slumping bank (caution).	0.88
9.89	Go along creek.	0.86
9.90	Switchback to R. **Junction:** avoid trail of use on L.	0.85
9.98	**Junction:** old trail on R. Keep L.	0.77
10.19	Views.	0.56
10.23	Switchback down to R, then to L in 100'.	0.52
10.30	Switchback to R, then to L in 85'.	0.45
10.40	Switchback to R, then to L in 55'.	0.35
10.44	Cross creek.	0.31
10.47	Top of rise.	0.28
10.48	**Junction:** avoid trail sharp R.	0.27
10.49	Begin partly rocky descent into Tonto Creek valley.	0.26
10.62	Cross *Tonto Creek* (6,090').	0.13
10.64	**Junction:** trail from L; go R.	0.11
10.69	**Junction:** trail from R; keep L.	0.06
10.71	Switchback to L.	0.04
10.73	Switchback up to R.	0.02
10.75	**Junction:** Tonto Fish Hatchery Road, FR 289. Elevation 6,140' Babe Haught Trail [143] is up road to N.	0.00

[31] Highline Trail EAST to WEST

Tonto Creek [FR 289] to Washington Park [FR 32A]

Introduction. This is a *very long section* of trail between access points; it is 9.6 miles just between FR 144, a rough 4WD road, and the Tonto Fish Hatchery. For day hikers, a section can be done via the Myrtle Trail and Babe Haught Trails if 2 cars are used on the Rim Road [FR 300], or using a 4WD, accessing rough FR 144. The section that was burned in the 1990 and 2002 fires is subject to blowdowns which can slow travel considerably.

The Dude Fire. From east of Washington Park near Dude Creek all the way to east of FR 289, almost all the way to Horton Spring, the area below the Rim was burned. This will affect travel through the area for many years to come. The fire began from a lightning strike on June 25, 1990, during a period of drought, low humidity, and very high temperatures, and quickly became an inferno. At the time this was the largest fire in Arizona history. Why was this fire so much worse than others? The explanations include the weather conditions, the large accumulations of fuel due to the prevention of the spread of previous fires in an area in which they are natural, and little thinning of the forest (greater than ideal density). By the time the fire was contained 10 days later, over 24,000 acres had been burned, most of it in the Tonto National Forest, but some in the Coconino and Apache-Sitgreaves Forests. Six lives were lost along with cattle, wildlife, and 36 million board feet of lumber. Over 1,100 people had to be evacuated. Since vegetation holding topsoil was burned, subsequent rains washed much of it away. Salvage logging, re-seeding, tree planting, fencing to prevent cattle from eating the sprouting new vegation are some of the rehabilitation steps that have been taken.[1] The fire's aftermath can be expected to continue to present problems in Highline Trail and side-trail maintenance. (In June of 2002 the even worse Rodeo-Chediski Fire raged out of control near the Rim and forced the evacuation of many more people.)

Famous Western novelist (56 in all) Zane Grey's cabin[2] was burned in the Dude Fire, but efforts of the Zane Grey Cabin Foundation will lead to a rebuilding of a replica at the site of the Rim Country Museum in Payson.

Maps. *Our Maps 7-12 (Highline 7 to Highline 12).* The USGS 1:24,000 Kehl Ridge and Dane Canyon quadrangles (1972) cover part of the trail route. On the Dane Canyon map much of the route is still correct. On Kehl Ridge, the trail location descending to the East Verde River is changed.

Access. *At the eastern end,* from FR 289 at the Hatchery Trailhead, 4.8 miles north of SR 260. This is 16.7 miles east of Payson [distance may change with highway re-alignment]. *At the western end* from Washington Park on FR 32A, 0.5 mile off FR 32, 3.3 miles from the Control Road [FR 64]. *Note that in wet weather the lower end of FR 32A may be muddy and impassable.*

---

[1] We wish to acknowledge the assistance of the Forest Service's publication *The Story of Dude Fire*, published 5/91.
[2] It was on the National Register of Historic Places.

General Description. From FR 289, easy side-hilling with some views leads past FR 289C, site of the Zane Grey cabin, along a relatively gradual slope of the Rim and over Roberts Mesa. There are several viewpoints. The trail then descends the side of the valley of Ellison Creek and and follows it up for 1.5 miles to the Myrtle Trail at 7.7 miles. Along the Rim's flank again, FR 144 (rough 4WD) is crossed at 9.6 miles. Valleys of Perley, Bonita, Fuller, and Dry Dude Creeks are crossed to Dude Creek at 13.6 miles. The final section approaches the broad valley of the East Verde River which is crossed at just over 16 miles; the trailhead is just beyond. Total elevation gain is 1,680' to FR 144 and an additional 740' to Washington Park, a total of about 2,400'.

The Tonto Creek Hatchery is worth a visit. It was built on the old Babe Haught homestead in 1935 by the Works Progress Administration [WPA]. It was rebuilt after a disastrous flood in 1970, and completely rebuilt in 1989 along with a visitor center and self-guided tour. 250 thousand catchable trout are produced annually.[3]

Read Down ↓	Detailed Trail Description	Read Up ↑
0.00	From the parking area at Tonto Fish Hatchery [FR 289], head W at sign, switchbacking up (elev. 6,120'). Switchback L in 40', ascending steadily.	16.09
0.04	Top of rise.	16.05
0.08	Turn R, descend.	16.01
0.11	Switchback to R, ascending.	15.98
0.15	Cross rocky small wash. Turn L and ascend.	15.94
0.20	Top of rise; level, with views.	15.89
0.24	Go over rocks.	15.85
0.31	Top of rise.	15.78
0.39	Cross open rock area.	15.70
0.41	Cliff area.	15.68
0.43	Leave edge, head R, ascending gradually.	15.66
0.44	Top of rise.	15.65
0.46	Cross open rocks with fine views.	15.63
0.48	**Junction:** leave vehicleway by descending L, following along rocks. Use care finding route, which is not always obvious.	15.61
0.50	Trail narrows, enters forest (unburned) area.	15.59
0.53	Cross more open rocks. Follow cairns and markers with care.	15.56
0.54	Descend to L, where way is not obvious.	15.57
0.59	**Important junction:** cross FR 259C (0.6 mi above FR 289). Just above on road is Zane Grey settlement (private). Near here was former Zane Grey cabin, burned in the 1990 Dude Fire.	15.50
0.71	Switchback to L over rocks for 145', then ascend, following cairns.	15.38
0.76	Hikers gate in barbed-wire fence.	15.33
0.80	Cross top of broad ridge, with views.	15.29
0.86	Reach edge of canyon; side-hill down into it. (There are many blow-downs.)	15.23
0.97	Switchback to L.	15.12
0.99	Cross creek.	15.10
1.07	Cross small wash; switchback to L.	15.02
1.09	Switchback to R (trail-of-use to L at bend).	15.00

[3]*Tonto Creek Hatchery.* Brochure [undated] produced by Arizona Game & Fish Dept., 2221 W. Greenway Rd., Phoenix 85023.

1.12	Bear L.	14.97
1.26	Electric fence (signs) on L. This will parallel or be close to the trail for some distance, but was in disrepair in 1997.	14.83
1.47	Cross small wash.	14.62
1.52	Swing R.	14.57
1.70	Turn R, descending steadily.	14.39
1.75	Cross small wash above.	14.34
1.79	Start ascent (for 100').	14.30
1.89	Top of rise. Start descent.	14.20
1.95	Switchback to L in heavy blow-down area.	14.14
1.96	Turn R.	14.13
1.99	Bottom of descent; cross wash.	14.10
2.04	Turn R.	14.05
2.05	Cross creek.	14.04
2.08	Go up steep pitch, then level, swinging to L, then to R.	14.01
2.36	Level off.	13.73
2.62	Enter treed area for 250'.	13.47
2.71	Top of rise on open rock; beautiful trail.	13.38
3.10	**Junction (5-way):** on L and half-R is vehicleway; on R is trail of use.	12.99
3.16	Bare hillside.	12.93
3.31	Top of rise.	12.78
3.34	Start descent. Views open to Mazatzals.	12.75
3.42	On brink of canyon; turn R and side-hill down.	12.67
3.45	Cross creek.	12.64
3.53	Top of rise.	12.56
3.55	Bottom of descent; ascend steadily.	12.54

3.63	Switchback to R.	12.46
3.66	Gate in barbed-wire fence (open). Turn L.	12.43
3.69	Top of ridge; fine views. Descend.	12.40
3.84	Turn L. In 55' turn R.	12.25
3.87	Top of rise.	12.22
3.95	Cross canyon and wash.	12.14
4.25	Top of rise.	11.84
4.4_	Cross open rocks.	11.66
4.40	Steep pitch.	11.69
4.45	Cross wash.	11.64
4.47	Top of rise.	11.62
4.71	Bottom of descent.	11.38
4.82	**Junction:** keep R where stock trail veers L.	11.27
5.13	Cross creek.	10.96
5.31	Go thru gate.	10.78
5.38	**Junction:** old vehicleway on L.	10.71
5.56	Top of rise.	10.53
5.60	Spring.	10.49
5.83	Cross creek near fence.	10.26
5.85	Top of rise.	10.24
6.24	Cross creek.	9.85
6.42	**Junction:** trail joins from L.	9.67
6.47	Cross creek.	9.62
6.50	**Junction:** keep L, follow cairns closely thru blowdown area.	9.59
6.59	**Junction:** go sharp R on vehicleway.	9.50
6.68	**Junction:** avoid trail R. Go downhill.	9.41
6.74	Cross creek.	9.35
6.78	**Junction:** vehicleway on R.	9.31
6.86	Top of rise.	9.23
6.89	Bottom of descent.	9.20
6.91	**Junction:** ignore trail on R.	9.18
7.32	Cross branch of Ellison Creek.	8.77
7.59	Turn R.	8.50
7.61	Bottom of descent.	8.48
7.68	**Important junction:** Myrtle Trail [30] on R (1.4 steep mi to Rim Road).	8.41
7.74	Gate (by-pass it).	8.35
7.83	Top of rise.	8.26
7.85	Bottom of descent.	8.24
7.91	Switchback to R.	8.18
7.97	Hiker's gate.	8.12
8.12	Hiker's gate.	7.97
8.37	**Junction:** ignore old vehicleway heading to R. Gate at top of rise.	7.72
8.51	Cross (dry) creek.	7.58
8.55	Top of rise.	7.54
8.57	Bottom of descent.	7.52
8.60	Hiker's gate.	7.49
8.65	Use care crossing open area where trail not well defined.	7.44
8.96	Top of rise.	7.13
9.01	Bottom of descent.	7.08
9.04	Top of rise after eroded section.	7.05
9.08	Hiker's gate.	7.01
9.20	Top of rise.	6.89
9.28	To L, hill with view is 170' off trail. In grassy area; use care finding trail.	6.81

9.31 Top of rise after switchback to L. 6.78
9.26 Switchback to R, to L in 100'. 6.83
9.46 Cross creek. 6.63
9.48 Bottom of descent. 6.61
9.51 Switchback to R. 6.58
9.53 Top of rise. 6.56
9.58 **Junction:** FR 144 [GPS 0481590/3805865]. This is a very rough 4WD road. ... 6.51
9.78 *Perley Creek* (perennial). 6.31
9.92 Top of rise. 6.17
9.95 Bottom of descent. 6.14
9.96 Top of rise. 6.13
10.01 Top of rise. 6.08
10.03 Top of rise. 6.06
10.05 Bottom of descent. Ascend steeply. 6.04
10.11 Top of rise. 5.98
10.14 Bottom of descent. 5.95
10.26 Top of rise. 5.83
10.34 Top of rise. 5.75
10.37 Top of rise. 5.72
10.42 Top of rise. 5.67
10.56 *Bonita Creek.* [GPS 0480485/3800265]. 5.53
10.92 **Junction:** NDT trail sharp R. 5.17
10.71 Pass (6,550'). 5.38
10.97 Hiker's gate. Views to W & S. 5.12
11.16 Steep pitch down. 4.93
11.22 Turn R. 4.87
11.23 Top of rise. 4.86
11.26 Cross old vehicleway. 4.83
11.55 *Fuller Creek* (often dry) [GPS 0489475/3806420]. Ascend steep, rocky pitch. 4.54
11.82 Top of rise. 4.27
11.90 Switchback to R. 4.19
11.92 Bottom of descent. 4.17
12.00 Top of rise. 4.09
12.09 **Junction:** trail of use on R. 4.00
12.11 Go around toe of minor ridge. 3.98
12.17 Cross to other side of valley. 3.92
12.33 Steep pitch up. 3.76
12.48 Switchback to L, ascending. 3.61
12.54 Top of ridge. 3.55
12.59 Descend into valley. 3.50
12.62 Switchback to L. 3.47
12.89 Switchback to R. 3.20
12.67 *Dry Dude Creek.* [GPS 0489145/3807325] 3.42
12.88 Top of rise at barbed-wire fence; go R and through gate. 3.21
12.91 CAUTION! Leave vehicle-way on R. [GPS 0487430/3808040] 3.18
13.53 Switchback to R. 2.56
13.55 *Dude Creek.* [GPS 0488060/3800690] 2.54
13.57 Steep pitch up bank. 2.52
13.66 Switchback to L. 2.43
13.69 Pass. Trail changes to vehicleway. 2.40
13.86 Dip. 2.23
13.90 Cross flat rocks. 2.19
13.99 Top of rise. 2.10

14.00	Dip.	2.09
14.04	Top of rise.	2.05
14.21	**Important junction:** vehicleway L; bear R.	1.88
14.35	Top of rise.	1.74
14.45	Cross small creek in sag.	1.64
14.50	Switchback to L, then to R.	1.59
14.51	Sag.	1.58
14.62	Sag.	1.47
14.64	**Junction:** alternate trail sharp R.	1.45
14.85	Cross creek.	1.24
15.58	**Junction:** at top of rise on ridge, ignore NDT on L. Cairn marks wrong trail.	0.51
15.72	Switchback to R.	0.37
15.74	Sag.	0.35
15.86	**Junction:** Pump Station Trail [296] on L, to Pump House, 0.9 mi., requiring crossing of E Verde River [GPS 0486185/3809580] .	0.23
15.92	Top of rise.	0.17
16.02	Switchback to L, descend and cross E Verde River.	0.07
16.05	**Junction:** road to TH on L; keep R to continue on Highline Trail.	0.04
16.09	**Junction:** Washington Park TH just to L on FR 32A (6,080').	0.00

[31] Highline Trail EAST TO WEST

FR 32A (Washington Park) to FR 440 (Camp Geronimo)

Introduction. This section of the trail has much variety. The results of the Dude Fire can be seen around Bray Creek, but most of this area was little affected. It is a long return trip on foot, really not feasible without leaving a car at one end or the other.

Maps. *Our Maps 5-7 (Highline 5: Camp Geronimo, Highline 6: N Sycamore Creek, and Highline 7: Washington Park).* The USGS 1:24,000 Kehl Ridge Quadrangle (1972) covers part of the trail, some of it in an old and now incorrect location.

Access. *At the eastern end,* from Washington Park Trailhead at the end of FR 32A. *At the western end,* from FR 440 at Geronimo Trailhead, 2 miles north of the Control Road [FR 64].

General Description. From Washington Park Trailhead, the trail circles around to the west, passing the junction with the Col. Devin Trail [290] to the Rim, crosses a power line service road and then Mail Creek and a private road at 1 mile. Several additional named creeks are passed as the trail crosses the Rim's flank with occasional views and sections of fine forest: East Chase, West Chase, North Sycamore in a deep canyon at 5 miles, East Bray, and Bray Creek at 6.2 miles. The Poison Spring Trail [29] is reached at 7.4 miles and Bear Spring at 7.5 miles. A service road is then followed down into the Webber Creek Valley to FR 440 south of Camp Geronimo at 9.25 miles. Total ascent is 1,120'.

NOTE that Camp Geronimo hosts thousands of Scouts, and over time quite a number of non-system trails have developed. Be careful to stay on the main trails.

Read Down ↓	Detailed Trail Description	Read Up ↑
0.00	**Washington Park** Trailhead at end of FR 32A (6,250'); main trail is 100' beyond.	9.27
0.04	Corral on L.	9.23
0.05	**Important junction:** Col. Devin Trail [290] ascends to R, 2 miles to FR 300.	9.22
0.06	**Junction:** trail of use on R.	9.21
0.13	Switchback to R.	9.24
0.17	Top of rise.	9.10
0.27	**Junction:** cross power line service road.	9.00
0.77	Bottom of descent.	8.40
0.94	Turn L; use care with alternate route.	8.33
0.96	Cross *Mail Creek*, and then private road.	8.31
1.00	Switchback to L.	8.27
1.20	Switchback to L, then to R in 250'.	8.07
1.83	Cross creek (water).	7.44
1.90	Eroded section.	7.37
1.91	Switchback to R (trenched, eroded).	7.36
1.97	Top of rise.	7.30
1.99	Landmark: double-trunked large alligator juniper tree.	7.28

5.84	Switchback to R.	3.43
6.19	Switchback to L.	3.08
6.22	*Bray Creek* in big valley (sign).	3.05
6.30	Bottom of descent.	2.97
6.33	Top of rise.	2.94
6.43	Bottom of descent. Leave area of Dude Fire.	2.84
6.46	Top of rise (6,310').	2.81
6.55	Rock spires above on R.	2.72
6.59	Top of rise on shoulder of ridge (6,220').	2.68
6.66	Switchback to R.	2.61
6.78	Top of rise.	2.49
6.79	Cross wash.	2.48
6.81	Eroded trail for 80'.	2.46
6.88	Top of rise (6,190').	2.39
6.97	Top of rise (6,240').	2.30
7.11	Switchback to L.	2.16
7.12	Top of rise.	2.15
7.26	Bottom of descent.	2.01
7.37	**Important junction:** Poison Spring Trail [29] uphill on R (to spring in 0.5 mi). Water may not be available.	1.90
7.41	Top of rise.	1.86
7.48	**Junction:** service road sharp R.	1.79
7.50	**Junction:** at top of rise and gate, Bear Spring area on L. BSA's Rim View Trail [undesignated] goes R (6,040'). Downhill is stock tank.	1.77
7.70	**Junction:** original trail sharp R.	1.57
7.73	Open area, use care.	1.54
7.74	Turn L.	1.53
7.77	**Junction:** trail splits, avoid trail sharp L.	1.50
7.79	Viewpoint (6,100'). Service road on R.	1.48
7.88	**Junction:** trail of use sharp R.	1.39
7.97	Cross creek.	1.30
8.06	Cross small creek.	1.21
8.07	Top of rise.	1.20
8.24	Viewpoint to L (5,810').	1.03
8.35	Cross dry creek.	0.92
8.53	**Junction:** trail of use on L.	0.74
8.60	**Junction (4-way):** trails of use cross.	0.67
8.62	**Junction:** two trails of use on R within 30'.	0.65
8.66	**Junction:** trail of use on R. Service road on R parallels trail.	0.61
8.67	Switchback L.	0.60
8.68	**Junction:** alternate trail rejoins.	0.59
8.69	**Junction:** trail of use on L.	0.58
8.70	Switchback R.	0.57
8.76	Cross small creek.	0.51
8.87	Top of rise (5,580'). Dirt service road parallels trail on R.	0.40
8.88	**Junctions:** many trails of use in this area.	0.39
9.04	Junction: trail-of-use on R.	0.23
9.07	Junction: trail-of-use on R.	0.20
9.11	Top of rise (5,480').	0.16
9.13	Junction: trail to R to Camp Geronimo.	0.14
9.16	**Junction:** trail of use on L.	0.11
9.27	Geronimo Trailhead (5,420').	0.00

[31] Highline Trail EAST to WEST

Geronimo Trailhead [FR 440] to Pine Trailhead

Introduction. The Boy Scouts of America's Camp Geronimo Trailhead is the start of this long 8-mile section to Pine Trailhead off SR 87. The flank of the Rim is followed up and down. This trip can be broken by side-trails at several points. In places the footway is rough, and careful planning is needed for through trips on foot.

Maps. *Our Maps 2, 3 & 5 (Highline 2: Pine, Highline 3: Milk Ranch Point,* and *Highline 5: Camp Geronimo).* The USGS 1:24,000 Pine quadrangle (1973) covers the terrain but shows only part of the trail and none of its side-trails. The Tonto National Forest map (2001) shows this section.

Access. *At the eastern end,* from FR 440, 2 miles north of the Control Road [FR 64]. *At the western end,* from SR 87, 0.5 mile south of Pine or 14.2 miles north of the junction of SR 87 and SR 260 in Payson, take a paved road 0.2 mile to the trailhead at a highway sign. Note: the trailhead area was heavily damaged by beetle infestations and has been selectively logged.

General Description. This trail leaves FR 440 and crosses Webber Creek (may be difficult after wet weather), ascending gradually, then steadily out of the valley, pasing the Geronimo Trail [240] that gives access to a number of trails up Milk Ranch Point and the Webber Creek Valley, and reaching the flank of the Rim at 0.6 mile. It then goes along the flank, passing several creek valleys with some views at about the 5,800' level, to Pine Spring at 3.25 miles. Red Rock Spring and the Red Rock Spring Trail [294] are reached at 4.5 miles. There are some very fine areas with views. The high point with a good viewpoint is at 5.8 miles. After a 450' descent in 2/3 of a mile, the Donahue Trail [27] branches off to Milk Ranch Point and there is a further gradual descent, passing the Pineview [28] and Pine Canyon [26] Trails to Pine Trailhead at 8 miles. Total elevation gain is 1,280'.

Read Down ↓	Detailed Trail Description	Read Up ↑
0.00	Leave FR 440 (2 mi N of Control Road [FR 64]) near the parking area (5,420').	8.04
0.01	Cross main branch of Webber Creek.	8.03
0.03	Cross secondary branch of Webber Creek.	8.01
0.07	**Junction:** trail of use to L. Keep R.	7.97
0.14	Cross vehicleway.	7.90
0.21	Cross creek.	7.83
0.31	Cross old vehicleway. Ascend.	7.73
0.36	**Junction:** Geronimo Trail [240] on R (to West Webber [228], Turkey Springs [217], and East Webber [289] Trails). Start steady 200' ascent.	7.68
0.41	Turn L.	7.63
0.64	Reach crest (5,750').	7.40
0.76	Cross creek after 4 small ones.	7.28
0.87	Top of rise (5,710'). Descend rocky trail.	7.17
0.91	Switchback to L.	7.03
0.98	Switchback to L.	6.96

1.08 Ascend steadily to S. 6.86
1.11 Top of rise. 6.83
1.19 Top of rise. Very scenic route. 6.75
1.27 Top of rise. 6.67
1.30 Pass rocks on R on steep descent with some erosion. 6.64
1.31 Bottom of descent. 6.63
1.42 Views open. 6.52
1.49 Enter forest, cross small creek. 6.45
1.55 Switchback to R on ascent. 6.39
1.63 Top of rise 6.31
1.80 Top of rise 6.14
1.91 Cross small washes. 6.03
2.01 Start ascent. 5.93
2.13 Top of rise. 5.81
2.20 Start descent. 5.74
2.27 Bottom of descent. Cross very small wash (5,920'). 5.67
2.56 Start descent. 5.38
2.59 Cross creek. 5.35
2.74 Top of rise (5,860'). 5.20
2.78 Cross flood plain and wash. 5.16
2.88 Top of rise (5,900'). 5.06
3.18 Top of rise. (6,030'). 4.76
3.24 Cross creek with beautiful pools. 4.70
3.27 Gate [open] at Pine Spring in wet area. 4.67
3.30 Top of rise in pleasant area in the pines. Ignore game trails to R. Side-hill into
      canyon. 4.64
3.41 Top of rise, viewpoint. 4.53
3.44 Bottom of descent. 4.50
3.50 Top of rise. 4.38
3.57 Cross creek and seeps. Use care in muddy, trenched area. 4.37
3.65 Top of rise (6,000'). 4.29
3.74 Top of rise. 4.20
3.90 Top of rise; descend. 4.04
3.92 Cross small creek. 4.02
4.00 Bottom of descent. 3.94
4.08 Top of rise. 3.86
4,15 Cross creek (5,900'). 3.79
4.31 Bottom of descent. 3.73
4.46 **Junction:** on L is Red Rock Spring Trail [294], leading down 1 mi to Control
      Road [FR 64], 2.5 mi E of SR 87. Elevation 6,000' 3.58
4.49 Box spring for stock on L. 3.55
4.52 Seep. In 70' leave Red Rock Spring area. 3.52
4.55 Spring. 3.49
4.61 Top of rise (6,080'). 3.43
4.72 Cross sag. 3.32
4.75 Cross creek in valley. 3.29
4.79 Top of rise. 3.25
4.83 Top of rise (6,040'). 3.21
4.85 Small sag. 3.19
4.97 Top of rise (views). 3.07
5.02 Top of rise. 3.02
5.04 Cross small sag. 3.00
5.13 Top of rise. 2.91

5.16	Top of rise in attractive area (6,220').	2.88
5.28	Descend steadily.	2.76
5.33	Switchback to L, then to R in 100'.	2.71
5.36	Turn L in valley.	2.68
5.46	Cross main branch of creek in broad, pleasant valley (6,150').	2.58
5.52	Top of rise (6,190').	2.52
5.56	Bottom of descent.	2.48
5.67	Top of rise (6,220').	2.37
5.76	Top of rise; views (6,270').	2.28
5.80	Top of rise; good viewpoint.	2.24
5.89	Top of rise on subsidiary ridge (6,250').	2.15
5.91	Turn L, level off in scenic area.	2.13
6.02	Turn R, off crest (use care here) (6,160').	2.02
6.06	Switchback to L.	1.98
6.13	Switchback to L, then to L again in 100'.	1.91
6.17	Switchback to R. on descent (6,010').	1.87
6.22	Bear L, then L again in 250'.	1.82
6.31	Turn R.	1.73
6.32	Switchback to L.	1.72
6.35	Bottom of descent.	1.69
6.40	Start ascent.	1.64
6.49	**Junction:** Donahue Trail [27] turns R and ascends steeply to Milk Ranch Point in 1.1 mi, to FR 218 in 2.6 mi. Elevation here 5,880'.	1.55
6.53	Switchback to R.	1.51
6.63	Switchback to R.	1.41
6.78	**Junction:** on L is poor vehicleway just before barbed-wire fence (there are 2 more connections with this vehicleway nearby).	1.26
6.94	Cross creek; beyond is **junction:** on R in small open area is Pineview Trail [28] to Pine Canyon Trail [26] in 0.7 mi.	1.10
7.14	Turn away from creek.	0.90
7.22	Cross creek.	0.82
7.62	Descend.	0.42
7.89	**Junction:** avoid trail bearing L to stock tank.	0.15
7.98	**Junction:** on R is Pine Canyon Trail [26]. On it 0.6 mi is the junction with the Pineview Trail [28]. Parallel creek bed, descending.	0.06
7.99	Bottom of descent.	0.05
8.01	Pass thru gate in barbed-wire fence, descend gradually.	0.03
8.04	Pine Trailhead (5,400'). Ample parking area, corral, toilet. Trail [16], Walnut Trail, leaves on opposite side of parking area and is continuation of Arizona Trail. This fire-damaged area was logged in 2003.	0.00

Highline Trail

Side Trails

[26] Pine Canyon Trail SOUTH to NORTH

Highline Trail [31] to Good Enough Trail

Introduction. The first section of this old trail is pleasant walking; the second portion is a steep ascent up an old vehicleway (quite exposed in hot weather) past Dripping Springs. The springs were developed years ago and unfortunately the areas are quite messy.

Maps. *Our Map 2 (Highline 2: Pine).* The USGS 1:24,000 Pine quadrangle (1973) shows only part of this trail section accurately.

Access. *At the southern end,* from the Pineview Trail [28] 0.7 mile from Pine Trailhead. Take the Highline Trail 335' to the junction, then turn left on the Pineview Trail (keep left). *At the northern end,* from the Good Enough Trail, 0.8 mile from Manzanita Trailhead.

General Description. This trail heads north, crossing two creeks in a valley. It then joins a vehicleway, ascending steeply northeast, and reaches Lower Dripping Springs at 1.6 miles. Shortly thereafter it crosses a by-pass around a tricky slump to Upper Dripping Spring at 1.7 miles. This area can be very muddy. It then side-hills at about 6,200' to the junction at 2.1 miles. Total elevation gain is 700'.

Read Down ↓	Detailed Trail Description	Read Up ↑
0.00	From the **junction** on the Highline Trail [31] 335' from Pine Trailhead, head N. Elevation 5,400'.	2.11
0.50	**Junction:** Pineview Trail [28] heads R, uphill [0.65 mi to Highline Trail, 1.1 mi from Pine Trailhead]. (Elevation 5,520').	1.61
0.67	Descend.	1.44
0.69	Cross creek in valley.	1.42
0.76	Cross creek; ascend very steadily.	1.35
0.79	Ease grade of ascent.	1.32
0.90	**Junction:** join vehicleway, ascend to R.	1.21
0.55	**Junction:** trail of use heads N. Continue steeply up vehicleway, in open.	1.16
1.06	Ease grade of ascent.	1.05
1.19	Bear L, generally level.	0.92
1.59	Lower Dripping Springs in level area, concrete box on side. *NOTE:* the Forest Service prefers hikers and equestrians to ascend on trail prior to reaching Lower Dripping Springs. At the Springs, to find trail beyond, do not follow vehicleway; past concrete box, ascend R, up slope and over dead tree. (There are several routes here.) In about 60' turn R, then at 100' switchback to L.	0.52
1.64	Turn L, avoid trail of use on R.	0.47
1.65	Switchback to R, avoid trail of use straight ahead.	0.46
1.76	Switchback to L. Just beyond, preferred alternate route turns R, high up slope to avoid bad slump ahead. [This area was slated for improvement.]	0.45
1.71	Near opposite side of slump.	0.40
1.73	Upper Dripping Spring; very muddy area. (One alternate trail from opposite side of slump avoids muddy area.) Ascend steeply.	0.38
1.77	Ease grade of ascent.	0.34
1.79	**Junction:** ignore trail of use to R.	0.32

1.82	Sag.	0.29
1.86	Top of rise. Descend steep side-hill.	0.25
1.90	Cross very small wash, rise, then descend steadily.	0.21
2.00	Cross very small wash.	0.11
2.11	**Junction:** Good Enough Trail [non-system trail, not maintained by Forest Service] sharp L (elev. 6,160'). It is 0.8 mile down to Manzanita Trailhead.	0.00

[26] Pine Canyon Trail SOUTH to NORTH

Good Enough Trail to Mogollon Rim

Introduction. The second section of this trail is highly varied.

Maps. *Our Maps 1, 2 & 4 (Highline 1: Lower Pine Canyon; Highline 2: Pine; Highline 4: Upper Pine Canyon).* The USGS 1:24,000 Pine quadrangle (1973) shows the trail, mostly in the correct location.

Access. *At the southern end,* from the Good Enough Trail, 0.8 mile from Manzanita Trailhead, or 0.7 mile from Pine Trailhead and 1.6 miles on the first section of this trail, a total of 2.3 miles. *At the northern end,* from SR 87. From the junction with SR 260, it is 1.3 miles to FR 6038 on the right. You have to watch for this; there is no sign on the highway. Pass through a gate in the barbed-wire fence (close it behind you) and drive another 500' to a parking area. Here there is a trail post (no sign). The actual trail sign is just to the south, where the trail starts its descent.

General Description. This trail heads north, keeping generally to the 6,200' level for a mile, passing several valleys, then descends 100' and winds along the slope, finally descending to the valley at 2.6 miles. At the 5,750' level it heads northeast up Pine Canyon, following up the east side of the creek. It reaches a trail junction with unofficial trails (built by Camp Lo Mia) at the creek crossing at 3.9 miles, then crosses the creek, ascending through a pleasant valley bottom, then side-hilling to reach the start of the 9 switchbacks at 4.9 miles. Here it ascends steadily for 650', with good views, to the top of a promontory on the Rim, from whence it rises easily to the forest road at 6.2 miles and SR 87 at 6.25 miles. Total elevation gain is 1,730'.

Read Down ↓	Detailed Trail Description	Read Up ↑
0.00	From the (unsigned) junction with the Good Enough Trail, 0.8 mi from Manzanita Trailhead, head N. Elevation 6,140'.	6.24
0.02	Round valley; ascend.	6.22
0.04	Top of rise.	6.20
0.18	Cross valley.	6.06
0.20	Start steep ascent over loose rock (use care).	6.04
0.22	Switchback to R. Continue ascent, then top out on crest with views.	6.02
0.29	Top of rise; start descent.	5.95
0.33	Descend steadily to R toward deep canyon.	5.91
0.35	Cross bottom of valley.	5.89
0.45	Cross minor sag.	5.79

0.46	Cross wash; ascend.	5.78
0.66	Cross major canyon (6,140'). Follow up hogback between two valleys.	5.58
0.73	Cross subsidiary canyon.	5.51
0.75	Top of rise (6,220').	5.49
0.80	Top of rise on plateau.	5.44
0.98	Cross small wash.	5.26
1.02	Views of Pine.	5.22
1.31	Turn L (W) down rim of major canyon. Switchback to R in 25'.	4.93
1.34	Cross bottom of canyon. There are beautiful colors here in the fall. Ascend steadily out of valley.	4.90
1.38	Top of rise. Descend to NW.	4.86
1.41	Turn R.	4.83
1.44	Cross major valley (6,000').	4.80
1.46	Top of rise. Descend, then ascend again.	4.78
1.51	Top of rise.	4.73
1.63	Top of rise. Start descent (6.080'), then level out to NE. Cross 3 small washes. .	4.61
1.79	Top of rise. Follow along for 430'.	4.45
1.87	Descend to NW.	4.37
1.95	Bottom of descent. Ascend briefly for 30', then drop briefly.	4.29
1.97	Sign "East Rim" and "Dripping Springs." In 25' pass thru barbed-wire fence.	4.27
2.08	Cross very small creek. Descend steadily to W.	4.16
2.44	Turn R (5,800').	3.80
2.47	Cross wash.	3.77
2.50	Top of rise; turn R.	3.74
2.58	Bottom of descent.	3.66
2.60	**Junction:** wide trail to L leads to locked gate at Camp LoMia in 295'. To R, trail [26] continues uphill [sign] Elevation here is 5,750'. *[This is 4.7 mi from Pine Trailhead.]*	3.64
2.70	Top of rise.	3.54
2.75	**Junction:** spur trail 40' L to Pine Creek. Continue on level trail.	3.49
2.81	Start ascent.	3.43
3.03	Cross very small wash, ascend, swinging R, the L.	3.21
3.09	Top of rise (5,840'). Level out.	3.15
3.30	Trail narrows, ascends.	2.94
3.34	Cross small wash.	2.90
3.38	**Junction:** non-system trail L, signs to "Tiny Cave" and "The Cave." Swing R and ascend.	2.86
3.42	Turn L, ease (5,940').	2.82
3.46	Top of rise; descend gradually.	2.78
3.49	Viewpoint over creek below.	2.75
3.55	**Junction:** non-system trail L, sign to "Temple Canyon 11/2 miles to St. Rt. 87." Continue straight ahead.	2.69
3.60	Beside creek.	2.64
3.81	Open area.	2.43
3.88	**Junction:** unofficial trails continuing up the creek bank are to "Deep Pools Canyon - 2 miles" and "Waterfall Canyon - 2 miles." *[This is 6 mi from Pine Trailhead.]* Descend.	2.36
3.89	Cross Pine Creek.	2.35
4.35	Cross creek valley.	1.89
4.36	Sign "Cinch Hook Butte 11/2 miles to St. Rt. 87" However, there is no clear trail to be found.	1.88
4.51	Sign "Spradling Canyon 11/2 miles to St. Rt. 87" However, there is no clear trail to be found.	1.73

4.56	Cross side-wash.	1.68
4.84	Round small valley.	1.40
4.94	Switchback to L (6,440'). Use care with steep, loose rock.	
	Sign "Switchbacks, 2 mi to St. Rt. 87" [wrong].	1.30
4.97	Switchback to R (6,470'), then to L in 100'.	1.27
5.01	Switchback to R (6,510').	1.23
5.16	Switchback to L.	1.08
5.27	Switchback to R (6,690').	0.97
5.36	Switchback to L at edge of steep drop-off (viewpoint).	0.88
5.43	Switchback to R at beautiful, shady ponderosa.	0.81
5.47	Switchback to L (6,880').	0.77
5.56	Switchback to R.	0.68
5.58	Switchback to L. Ascend with loose rock.	0.66
5.63	Switchback to R (7,030').	0.61
5.67	Switchback to L, at crest; end of promontory.	0.57
5.92	**Junction:** join vehicleway, turn R.	0.32
6.01	**Junction:** keep L where vehicleway joins sharp R thru fence.	0.23
6.11	Start final ascent.	0.13
6.24	**Junction:** FR 6038, parking area (7,240'). For SR 87, head N thru barbed-wire fence for 500'. *[This is 8.4 mi from Pine Trailhead.]*	0.00

[28] Pineview Trail

Introduction. This short connector makes a nice low-level circuit trip using the Highline [31] and Pine Canyon [26] Trails. There are a few views.

Maps. *Our Map 2 (Highline 2: Pine).* The USGS 1:24,000 Pine quadrangle (1973) does not show this trail.

Access. From the Highline Trail [31] 1.1 miles east of Pine Trailhead, or from the Pine Canyon Trail at 0.5 mile.

General Description. After leaving the Highline Trail, it crosses a semi-open plateau and then descends steadily to end at the Pine Canyon Trail at 0.7 mile. Total elevation loss is 140'.

Read Down ↓	Detailed Trail Description	Read Up ↑
0.00	From the Highline Trail [31] (5,660') 1.1 mi E of Pine TH, turn sharp L (W).	0.65
0.05	Open area.	0.60
0.28	Turn NW, then N. descend with views.	0.37
0.40	Open area to R.	0.25
0.47	Descend SW.	0.18
0.65	Trail ends at Pine Canyon Trail [26] (L 0.5 mi to Highline Trail near Pine TH). Elevation 5,520'.	0.00

[16] Oak Spring Trail   EAST to WEST

[Part of the Arizona Trail]

Pine Trailhead to Walnut Trail [251]

Introduction.   The trails west of Pine Trailhead are less used than the Highline Trail, but the first section of this trail is now part of the Arizona Trail, the first link between the Highline Trail and the approach southwards to the Mazatzals. The countryside is attractive, with some varied terrain and views, but not spectacular.

Maps. *Our Map 19 (AZ Trail East: Pine/Strawberry).* The USGS 1:24,000 Buckhead Mesa and Pine quadrangles (1973) cover the approaches but do not show the trail.

Access. At the eastern end, from Pine Trailhead off SR 260, 1.7 miles north of Control Road. At the western end, from the Walnut Canyon Trail [251] 1.7 miles south of FR 428 (Hardscrabble Road).

General Description. The Oak Spring Trail leaves Pine Trailhead and crosses SR 87 in half a mile, descending gradually across an area with some cabins until it crosses a creek at 1.3 miles and ascends, passing Bradshaw Tank at 1.75 miles. It then rises over a shoulder, up and down, with some views, dropping some 250' to meet the Walnut Trail [251] at 3.75 miles in Oak Spring Canyon, where this trail ends.

Read Down ↓	Detailed Trail Description	Read Up ↑
0.00	From Pine Trailhead, head SE	0.50
0.50	Cross SR 87.	0.00
0.00	From SR 87 crossing (5,420'), head SSE, level.	3.24
0.05	Pass thru gate, descend gradually to W, then NW.	3.19
0.25	Level off.	2.99
0.41	Cross moderate creek (bouldery); head W, descending gradually.	2.83
0.46	Tonto National Forest property boundary on L.	2.78
0.49	**Junction:** with power line ahead, bear L (SW). In 235' cross under it.	2.75
0.55	**Junction:** continue straight ahead on vehicle way.	2.69
0.58	**Junction (4-way):** turn L, crossing creek in 40'.	2.66
0.59	**Junction:** bear R.	2.65
0.61	**Junction:** Switchback to L; keep R on vehicle way.	2.63
0.65	Bear R down bank on trail.	2.59
0.66	**Junction:** rejoin vehicle way in flat area.	2.58
0.68	**Junction:** keep R at sign on trail.	2.56
0.77	Camping area on L; cross minor creeks.	2.47
0.80	Cross creek. Head NW with care for route.	2.44
0.85	Ascend thru attractive area, to W.	2.39
0.91	Cross very small wash, ascend steeply for 435'.	2.33
1.07	Level.	2.17
1.12	Gate in barbed-wire fence; go thru it, then parallel it briefly; then go thru another gate.	2.12

1.16	Descend in rocky area, pass over rocks.	2.08
1.19	Switchback to L at barbed-wire fence, then bear R, crossing wash.	2.05
1.26	Pass alongside Bradshaw Tank.	1.98
1.52	Descend to major creek (5,400'). Ascend to W, then to SW.	1.72
2.11	On plateau (5,620').	1.13
2.30	Trail narrows.	0.94
2.33	Turn R (important turn - use care). Descend to SW.	0.91
2.36	Turn R across rock (caution), descending.	0.88
2.38	Bear L, then R in 90'.	0.86
2.40	Level.	0.84
2.42	Cross small creek., then ascend steadily	0.82
2.47	Top of rise (5,540'). Start rocky descent. Canyon in view ahead.	0.77
2.52	Descend steeply, switchback to R (W).	0.72
2.53	Switchback to L, then to R in 45', then turn L.	0.71
2.55	Cross small creek in draw.	0.69
2.59	Top of rise (5,470').	0.65
2.63	Side-hill with fine views to S.	0.61
2.74	Bottom of descent (5,390'). Level briefly, then descend gradually with views.	0.50
2.82	Switchback to L, descending to SE.	0.42
2.91	Switchback to R, then 6 more on descent.	0.33
3.12	Bottom of descent (5,180'); follow creek.	0.12
3.13	Leave creek, ascend steep bank.	0.11
3.17	Top of rise; descend gradually to S.	0.07
3.24	**Junction:** trail [251] heads R (NW), 2.68 mi to FR 428 (5,290'). To L is Walnut Trail [251], the Arizona Trail continuation *[3.74 mi from Pine TH]*.	0.00

[27] Donahue Trail   SOUTH to NORTH

Highline Trail [31] to Milk Ranch Point

Introduction. Like many of the trails ascending the Rim, this is steep with lots of switchbacks and loose rock, but fine views. It is not suitable for horses.

Maps. *Our Maps 2 & 3 (highline 2: Pine, and Highline 3: Milk Ranch Point).* The USGS 1:24,000 Pine quadrangle (1973) covers the terrain but does not show the trail.

Access. *At the southern end,* from the Highline Trail [31] at 1.6 miles east of Pine Trailhead. *At the northern end,* take FR 300 from SR 260 for 0.1 mile to FR 218A, turn right for 1.3 miles to FR 218 on Milk Ranch Point; continue right onto Milk Ranch Point. (The full road approach requires a 4WD vehicle.)

General Description. This trail has a relentless 1.1 mile, 31-switchback ascent to the Rim, with loose rock, obviously not recommended for horses or mountain-bikes. Views are excellent. It then ascends further up Milk Ranch Point (in forest) at a lesser grade to 2.6 miles. Total elevation gain is 1,640'.

Geology. The Donahue Trail [misspelled "Donohue"] is described in Ivo Luchitta's book *Hiking Arizona's Geology*, 2001, pp. 83-87. The Rim is the boundary between the Colorado Plateau and the Arizona Transition Zone, the latter having much more complex structure of ranges, valleys, and basins. The lavas that cap Milk Ranch Point are of Miocene Age (about 14 million years old). They protected an older and more southern rim from the forces that moved the edge northward. There are still controversies over the formation of the Rim. Along the trail one can see rocks with a reddish color from Pennsylvanian and Permian beds that are roughly the age of the Supai formation in the Grand Canyon.

Read Down ↓	Detailed Trail Description	Read Up ↑
0.00	From the Highline Trail 1.55 mi E of Pine Trailhead, head NE, ascending. Sections are rocky and eroded. (Elevation 5,880').	2.63
0.14	Switchback to L (first of a total of 31!).	2.49
0.61	Trenched section.	2.02
0.86	Brief level stretch for 135'.	1.77
1.10	Crest of Rim (6,690'). Views start.	1.53
1.36	Viewpoint on L, just off trail, over Pine and the distant Mazatzals; very pleasant walking.	1.27
1.53	Leave Rim area, where there are fine camping areas; head NNE.	1.10
1.63	Ascend steadily.	1.00
1.70	Head N.	0.93
1.81	Switchback to L (NNW).	0.82
1.83	Ease, head NNE.	0.80
1.84	Ascend N, then NE.	0.79
2.10	**Junction:** join old vehicleway (7,160'). Ascend to NE.	0.53
2.14	Sign "Donahue Trail #27".	0.49
2.23	**Junction:** vehicleway [FR 9380]. Go L on it.	0.40
2.30	Ease.	0.33

2.35	Bear R (E).	0.28
2.46	Bear L (NE).	0.17
2.63	**Junction:** FR 218 (Elevation 7,270'). This trail ends.	0.00

[294] Redrock Spring Trail EAST to WEST

Control Road [FR 64] to Highline Trail [31]

Introduction. Redrock Spring was used by both Apaches and later settlers as a watering hole. This trail was used to move cattle from Buckhead Mesa (to the south) to the Highline Trail and over the Rim to summer range.

Maps. *Our Map 3 (Highline 3: Milk Ranch Point).* The USGS 1:24,000 Buckhead Mesa quadrangle (1973) covers the approach but does not show the trail.

Access. *At the eastern end,* from Control Road [FR 64], 2.5 miles east of SR 87. *At the western end,* from the Highline Trail [31] 3.6 miles east of Pine Trailhead and 4.5 miles west of FR 440.

General Description. This trail is an important access route, being just under a mile long. It ascends an old vehicleway to a plateau at 0.4 mile, then ascends a rocky slope to the Highline Trail at 1 mile, with some views. Total elevation gain is 610'.

Read Down ↓	*Detailed Trail Description*	Read Up ↑
0.00	From Control Road [FR 64], 2.5 mi E of SR 87, trail starts at small parking area (sign). Elevation is 5,390'. Ascend steadily on old vehicleway.	0.98
0.44	Come onto plateau (5,540').	0.54
0.45	**Important junction:** ignore vehicleway on R.	0.53
0.47	**Junction:** [sign] leave vehicleway to R, still on plateau, start ascent.	0.51
0.50	Turn R. Trail gradually steepens. There is lots of loose rock.	0.48
0.98	**Junction:** Highline Trail [31]. There are several seeps in the area, and a stock tank is only 160' W. Red Rock Spring is 370' to the L (W). There are fine views S and E from here.	0.00

[228] West Webber Trail EAST to WEST

Turkey Springs Trail [217] to FR 218 on Milk Ranch Point

Introduction. This is an old pack trail with limited views, providing one side of a useful trail loop involving the Turkey Springs Trail [217].

Maps. *Our Maps 3 & 4 (Highline 3: Milk Ranch Point, and Highline 4: Upper Pine Canyon).* The USGS 1:24,000 Pine quadrangle (1973) does not accurately show the relatively new Geronimo Trail [240] around Camp Geronimo or the location of this trail.

Access. *At the eastern end,* from the Turkey Springs Trail [217], 0.1 mile from the Geronimo Trail [240] (a total of 2 miles from Geronimo Trailhead via the Highline Trail [31]). *At the western end,* from FR 218, 1.4 miles south of Turkey Springs Trail, and 5.1 miles from SR 87.

General Description. This trail leaves the Turkey Springs Trail at the tank and crosses a semi-open area, then starts ascending crossing several creek branches to start its major ascent at 1.1 miles. It then makes 28 switchbacks as it climbs a wide valley of a branch of Webber Creek. It tops out at the Rim's edge at 2.2 miles, reaching FR 218 at 2.3 miles. For those hiking the descent, note that there is no highway sign, but there is a cairn. There is a Forest Service sign 135' in from the road. Total elevation gain is 1,400'.

Read Down ↓	Detailed Trail Description	Read Up ↑
0.00	At the **junction** with the Turkey Springs Trail [217] at a tank (5,780'), wide trail ascends.	2.27
0.13	**Junction:** old vehicleway ascends straight ahead (reaches Turkey Spring Trail [217] in 500'); at sign, keep L (5,800') .	2.14
0.20	Cross very small wash, continue in semi-open area.	2.07
0.24	Clearing.	2.03
0.46	Blowdown.	1.81
0.52	Cross side-creek, then switchback to R.	1.75
0.62	Start ascent.	1.65
0.85	Cross large side-creek [water pipes in area] (6,030'). Ascend SW.	1.42
1.09	Cross major creek (6,150').	1.18
1.13	Go around blow-down.	1.14
1.26	**Junction:** signboard (not by USFS) indicates trail L "Milk Ranch Point West" (6,280'). (Descends to the Geronimo Trail.) On post is indicator for Trail [213] [wrong]. Keep R, continue ascending.	1.01
1.29	Start ascent, turn R.	0.98
1.32	Turn L.	0.95
1.35	Go around blow-down.	0.91
1.41	Switchback to R, then to L.	0.86
1.55	Switchback to R.	0.82
1.47	Switchback to L.	0.80
1.50	Switchback to R, then to L (6,500').	0.77
1.53	Switchback to R.	0.74
1.60	Switchback to L.	0.67
1.63	Switchback to R, then to L in 100'.	0.64

1.67	Switchback to R, then to L.	0.60
1.71	Switchback to R.	0.56
1.73	Switchback to L.	0.54
1.76	Switchback to R; limited views here (7,780').	0.51
1.78	Switchback to L, then to R.	0.49
1.80	Switchback to L (canyon on R).	0.47
1.82	Switchback to R.	0.45
1.84	Switchback to L.	0.43
1.86	Switchback to R, then to L. Make easy traverse to S.	0.41
1.89	Switchback to R.	0.38
1.93	Switchback to L.	0.34
1.98	Switchback to R, then to L.	0.29
2.01	Switchback to R.	0.26
2.03	Switchback to L, ascending steadily.	0.24
2.24	Reach edge of Rim, ease.	0.03
2.27	**Junction:** FR 218 L & R. Elevation 7,240'. To R on road, Turkey Springs Trail [217] is 1.44 mi. (It is 5.1 mi to SR 87.)	0.00

[289] East Webber Trail SOUTH to NORTH

Geronimo Trail [240] to Rim Base

Introduction. Upper Webber Creek provides a cool, shady area with springs flowing out of the base of the Rim. The lower part of the trail is fairly easy and relaxing; there are five major crossings of the creek, plus several of side-creeks. After prolonged wet weather, the trail may be impassable. The upper section becomes increasingly narrow, brushy, and rough.

Maps. *Our Map 5 (Highline 5: Camp Geronimo).* The USGS 1:24,000 Kehl Ridge quadrangle (1972) shows most of the trail, except for the section from the Geronimo Trail to Webber Creek.

Access. *At the southern end,* from the Geronimo Trail [240], elevation 5,760', 2.1 miles from Geronimo Trailhead. There is also access from Camp Geronimo (private).

General Description. From the junction at the end of the Geronimo Trail [240] at the Turkey Springs Trail [217], head east to the crossing of West Webber Creek at 0.2 mile and then the side-trail from Camp Geronimo at 1.1 miles. Shortly thereafter pleasant trail starts, leading on a gradual ascent through shady forest to 2.5 miles, from which point it becomes rougher. Towards its end, the valley walls close in and the trail clambers over logs and rocks to springs and seeps at 3.1 miles. Total elevation gain is 900'.

Read Down ↓	Detailed Trail Description	Read Up ↑
0.00	From the **junction** at the end of the Geronimo Trail [240] with Turkey Springs Trail [217], this trail ascends N, then E. (Elevation is 5,760'.)	3.14
0.09	Descend to N.	3.05
0.17	**Junction (4-way):** trail of use to R & L. Descend broader way (no sign).	2.97
0.21	Cross West Webber Creek (5,700'). Head E.	2.93
0.24	Top of rise; descend to E.	2.90
0.27	Bottom of descent.	2.87
0.31	Top of rise. Descend to N.	2.83
0.35	Cross wash; ascend to NW, then N.	2.79
0.50	Switchback to R (S), then head E in 125'.	2.64
0.61	Bottom of descent.	2.53
0.64	Top of rise; swing L.	2.50
0.67	Head E, then NE.	2.47
0.73	Views.	2.41
0.86	Bottom of descent. Swing R (E).	2.28
0.93	**Junction:** trail of use to R.	2.21
1.10	**Junction:** wide trail R leads to private Camp Geronimo [gate is 0.1 mi, Geronimo Trailhead is 1.35 mi.].	2.04
1.13	Top of rise.	2.01
1.15	Cross side-wash (rocky vehicleway).	1.99
1.21	**Junction:** where vehicleway continues, bear R into forest on narrow trail.	1.93
1.31	Bottom of descent. Rise gradually.	1.83
1.32	Top of rise. Descend to NE.	1.82
1.35	First Webber Creek crossing (5,720'). Ascend N.	1.79

1.39	Ease; head N at easy grade.	1.75
1.50	Top of rise; level out.	1.64
1.60	Cross Webber Creek (5,830').	1.54
1.65	Landmark: go between cut ends of large log across trail.	1.49
1.86	Cross large side-creek.	1.28
1.97	Level area beside side-creek.	1.17
2.01	Bear R.	1.13
2.02	Level, then descend.	1.12
2.05	Landmark: go between cut ends of large log across trail, then turn R in 25'.	1.09
2.09	Bottom of descent. Level walking.	1.05
2.14	Cross Webber Creek for 3rd time; keep along and above it on far side	1.00
2.20	Cross creek for 4th time; parallel it.	0.94
2.30	Cross side creek.	0.84
2.31	**Junction:** keep R (L ends).	0.83
2.41	Blow-down.	0.73
2.47	Descend steadily.	0.67
2.49	Cross Webber Creek for 5th (and last) time.	0.65
2.50	**Junction:** in flat clearing, non-system signs indicate "Rimview Trail" ascending steeply to R (said to be a steep, rough trail leading S to the Highline Trail [31]). Trail ascends steadily from here, and is narrower and progressively rougher.	0.64
2.60	Ease	0.54
2.69	Flat area.	0.45
2.72	Landmark: go over huge log.	0.42
2.74	Go around blow-down.	0.40
2.75	Go under log.	0.39
2.82	Top of rise.	0.32
2.84	Cross side creek (from R). A spring is across main creek bed on L.	0.30
2.97	Switchback to R, then to L, ascending steep pitch.	0.17
3.02	Huge blow-down (go over it).	0.12
3.06	Bottom of descent, on rocks.	0.08
3.08	**Junction:** L to pools near spring.	0.06
3.09	Cross side-creek.	0.05
3.10	Pools, seeps on L. In 30', go steeply up rougher trail.	0.04
3.14	Trail ends at spring emerging from base of Rim (6,550').	0.00

[240] Geronimo Trail SOUTH to NORTH

Highline Trail [31] to East Webber Trail [289] and
Turkey Springs Trail [217]

Introduction. The Geronimo Trail by-passes private property, giving access to several important trails. It also provides some good views.

Maps. *Our Maps 4 & 5 (Highline 4: Upper Pine Canyon, and Highline 5: Camp Geronimo).* The USGS 1:24,000 Pine and Kehl Ridge Quadrangles (1973 and 1972, respectively) cover the approach but do not show the trail.

Access. *At the southern end,* from the Highline Trail 1/3 mi west of Geronimo Trailhead. *At the northern end,* from the Turkey Springs Trail [217] or the East Webber Trail [289].

General Description. This trail is more rugged than apparent from the map, so allow extra time. Total elevation gain is about 500'. It runs up and down along the flank of the Rim, with occasional viewpoints, to give access to 3 other trails (at 1.4 miles and at the end at 1.8 miles).

Read Down ↓	Detailed Trail Description	Read Up ↑
0.00	From the Highline Trail [31] 0.36 mi W of Geronimo Trailhead at FR 440 (5,560'), diverge R, ascending gradually to the SW. Sign indicates "Turkey Springs 2, E Webber 3." Trail is an old vehicleway.	1.77
0.06	Top of rise; head W.	1.71
0.10	Cross wide, bouldery wash; start steady ascent in 50'.	1.67
0.13	Ease. Head NW on level. In 160' head W.	1.64
0.26	Steady, rocky ascent starts.	1.51
0.30	Top of rise (5,700'). Head WNW.	1.47
0.33	Cross wash, level out to NNW, then N.	1.44
0.38	Start steady ascent.	1.39
0.40	Edge; views open. Ascend WNW. Level off in 175' Swing to W.	1.37
0.51	Swing to SW.	1.26
0.54	Start rocky ascent.	1.23
0.62	Level off at 5,810'. Beautiful walking.	1.15
0.70	Viewpoint (5,800'). Descend steadily to N, then to NW.	1.07
0.83	Bottom of descent; swing R (NE).	0.94
0.87	Top of rise; descend gradually to NE.	0.90
0.90	**Junction:** keep L, ascending steeply (straight ahead is old vehicleway).	0.87
0.93	Top of rise (5,820'). Head W, descend, then to NW.	0.84
1.01	**Junction:** road sharp R blocked (re-entering vehicleway). Head W.	0.80
1.06	Bottom of descent. Ascend gradually to SW and S.	0.75
1.12	Switchback to R; ascend to N.	0.65
1.14	Top of rise. Descend to N.	0.63
1.23	Top of rise.	0.54
1.27	Bottom of descent. Ascend steadily to NW.	0.50
1.34	Top of rise (5,800').	0.43
1.36	**Junction:** trail of use descends on R (rejoins later.) Descend to W.	0.41
1.38	Turn R, downhill.	0.39
1.42	**Junction:** not very obvious cut-off trail on R.	0.35

1.44 **Junction:** Sign "Turkey Springs 1/4 mile; E Webber Trail 11/4 miles; Highline Trail 13/4 miles." Turn L here [gate on R]. 0.33

1.51 Cross creek in valley; ascend to NW, then to W. 0.26

1.59 **Junction:** unofficial trail on L to "Milk Ranch Point West." This meets the West Webber Trail along its course. 0.18

1.71 **Junction:** with creek ahead, take by-pass trail on L. 0.06

1.73 Cross major creek; in 25' rejoin eroded vehicleway. Ascend steadily to W. 0.04

1.77 **Junction:** This trail ends. Straight ahead is the Turkey Springs Trail [217] also to the West Webber Trail [228]. To the R is start of the East Webber Trail [289]. Elevation 5,760'. 0.00

[217] Turkey Springs Trail EAST to WEST

Geronimo Trail [240] to FR 218 on Milk Ranch Point

Introduction. Fine views to the east and south abound from this old pack trail. The first section leaves from the Geronimo Trail, the second from the junction with the West Webber Trail [228]. A good circuit can be made with the latter trail.

Maps. *Our Map 4 (Highline 4: Upper Pine Canyon).* The USGS 1:24,000 Pine quadrangle (1973) shows the trail, with only minor changes in recent years.

Access. *At the eastern end,* 1.8 miles from Geronimo Trailhead via the Highline [31] Trail and Geronimo [240] Trails, or 2.5 miles from FR 218 on Milk Ranch Point. *At the western end,* from FR 218, 5.1 miles from the junction of FR 300 & SR 87. FR 218A turns right just a little over 0.1 mile from that point, then follow it 1.3 miles to a junction with FR 218. Turn right on this good gravel road for 3.7 miles to FR 9381F. The actual trailhead is 275' in on this side-road. (There is no sign at FR 218. There is one 300' in on FR 9381F.)

General Description. This trail starts as an old vehicleway, but at 0.1 mile at Turkey Spring Tank (where the West Webber Trail [228] branches left) it becomes a trail that starts switchbacking at 0.5 mile and has 28 of these as it ascends on top of — or on the north side of — the ridge crest. There are fine views of the Rim to the north (the promontory east of West Webber Creek valley) and further east and south. Footway is generally good. Total elevation gain is 1,600'.

Read Down ↓	Detailed Trail Description	Read Up ↑
0.00	Trail starts at **junction** at end of Geronimo [240] and East Webber [289] Trails. Elevation 5,760'. Start steady ascent.	2.53
0.14	**Junction:** West Webber Trail branches L at Turkey Springs tank [may be empty]. Keep R, continuing ascent in forest.	2.39
0.28	**Junction (4-way):** this trail crosses an old vehicleway (sharp L 500' to West Webber Trail [228]) (5,800'); bear L, uphill.	2.25
0.47	Switchback to L (5,930').	2.06
0.51	Switchback to R. Views.	2.02
0.55	Switchback to L, then to R in 60', with views. Steady climb.	1.98
0.66	Switchback to R.	1.89
0.72	Turn L, ascend more steeply (views). Elevation 6,060'.	1.83
0.81	**Junction:** original trail, now blocked, ascends more steeply to L; ignore it.	1.74
0.89	Switchback to L (6,190') along R side of crest.	1.66
0.91	Switchback to R, then to L in 170'.	1.64
0.97	Switchback to R, then to L in 150'.	1.58
1.04	Old trail descends to L (blocked) where this trail switchbacks to R onto crest (6,290'). Ascend up rocky crest with views. Agaves and manzanita start.	1.51
1.13	Top of rise, descend for just 50', then ascend to R of crest.	1.42
1.22	Switchback to L.	1.33
1.27	Switchback to R at crest (6,490'). Keep to R of crest.	1.28
1.34	Steep pitch up for 40', then to L, heading SE in 200'.	1.21

1.43	Switchback to R on crest.	1.12
1.44	Ascend steadily (6,600').	1.11
1.48	Switchback to R, head to N.	1.07
1.51	Switchback to L.	1.04
1.54	Cross crest. Turn R, steeply up rocky trail.	1.01
1.61	Switchback to L, then to R in 30', to L in 150' more.	0.92
1.71	**Junction:** trail straight ahead leads to rock pinnacle in 100' [CAUTION: loose rock, steep drop-offs!]. This trail turns R and ascends.	0.82
1.78	Turn R.	0.75
1.85	Turn L, then R.	0.68
1.88	Switchback to R.	0.65
1.93	Edge of Rim (7,150).	0.60
1.95	Barbed-wire fence; gate [please close it after you].	0.58
2.03	Top of rise.	0.50
2.07	Bottom of descent.	0.46
2.13	Top of rise (7,240'). Descend to NW.	0.40
2.28	Bottom of descent. Turn L, ascend briefly over a rise, then head W.	0.25
2.48	**Junction:** at FR 9381F, turn R on it. (Sign just before joining road)	0.05
2.53	Trail ends at FR 218. To L, West Webber Trail [228] is 1.4 mi to S.	0.00

[29] Poison Spring Trail

Introduction. A short service road leads to a spring used as a water supply. Otherwise, there is little to recommend this as a separate trip.

Maps. *Our Map 5 (Highline 5: Camp Geronimo).* The USGS 1:24,000 Kehl Ridge quadrangle (1972) covers the approach and the trail, but its location is partly incorrect.

Access. From the Highline Trail [31] 1.9 miles east of Geronimo Trailhead or 7.4 miles west of Washington Park Trailhead.

General Description. The service road to the spring and its pipeline generally follows the jeep road, which climbs 60' to the north, then heads northeast to the spring, which is the water supply for Camp Geronimo (this road is the same one that parallels part of the Highline Trail from Camp Geronimo). There are camping possibilities near the spring; but if you do this, ensure that you are some distance away from it. Total elevation gain is 180'.

Read Down ↓	Detailed Trail Description	Read Up ↑
0.00	From the Highline Trail [31] (6,120'), turn L (N), ascending up rocky, wide trail.	0.48
0.19	Top of rise. Bear R (6,180').	0.29
0.24	Descend to N.	0.24
0.27	Bottom of descent. Ascend to R along pipeline.	0.21
0.36	Top of rise; go up and down.	0.12
0.45	Bear L, ascend.	0.03
0.48	Poison Spring (6,270'). Sign "Camp Geronimo Water Supply - Keep Out."	0.00

[290] Colonel Devin Trail SOUTH to NORTH

Highline Trail to Rim Road [300]

[Part of the Arizona Trail]

Introduction. This trail is named for Col. T. C. Devin, 8th Cavalry, who commanded and patrolled the Arizona District around 1868. The monument near the top (in the Coconino National Forest) commemorates the "Battle of Big Dry Wash" (really East Clear Creek) of July 17, 1882, the last battle of U.S. troops and the White Mountain Apaches.

Maps. *Our Maps 7 & 8 (Highline 7: Washington Park, and Highline 8: RR Tunnel).* The USGS 1:24,000 Kehl Ridge quadrangle (1972) covers part of the route of this trail, but not all of it, and the approach has changed.

Access. *At the southern end,* from the Highline Trail [31] 260' west of Washington Park Trailhead. *Road directions for this trailhead:* from Payson head north on SR 87, turning right at 0.8 mile onto Houston Mesa Road, which heads east. Pass Shoofly Ruins at 2.9 miles. Paving ends at 5.2 miles. The East Verde River is crossed on a bridge at 6.8 miles, then forded at 8.1 and 8.8 miles (at low water only, in standard vehicles). Pass through the Whispering Pines residential area at 9 miles, reaching the Control Road [FR 64] at 10 miles. Turn left on it for 0.7 mile, then right (north) onto FR 32 (0.0 mile). At 3.1 miles on this road enter private land (keep left). At 3.2 miles turn right, then immediately left, uphill. The trailhead is 1 mile further (total 4.2 miles from Control Road) through a beautiful camping area. Total distance from Payson, 13.8 miles. *At the northern end,* from the Rim Road [300] 11.4 miles east of its start at SR 87, or 29.9 miles west of SR 260.

General Description. This trail has the easiest grade of any trail ascending the Rim. It follows a power line (low-tension, no noise) most of the way, and a mostly buried aqueduct in its lower section. From the Washington Park Trailhead, head northwest at a sign for both trails, following the Highline Trail for 265' to a junction. Here the Col. Devin Trail starts, immediately ascending steadily on a rocky trail. After 0.2 mile it follows the west bank of the East Verde River (here a creek in its headwaters). There are two brief sections where the aqueduct is exposed. At 0.8 mile the power line is joined. At 1.5 miles the trail leaves the power line on newly constructed taril and ascends switchbacks to gain elevation above the valley. At 1.7 miles there is a junction with the Tunnel Trail (0.2 mile long). Continuing, the trail side-hills steadily up a rock shelf with expanding views to just under 2 miles, where it rejoins the power line and reaches the Rim Road at 2.1 miles. Total elevation gain is 1,200'.

Caution. The "Pack Rat Fire" (August 2002) had a major effect on this area. From just north of Washington Park Trailhead along the west side of the trail the area has been burned. This may increase the risk of blow-downs, erosion, and slides. (Check on whether it is suitable for equestrian use.)

Read Down ↓	Detailed Trail Description	Read Up ↑
0.00	From the Highline Trail [31] 265' NW of Washington Park TH, this trail starts N at a sign, paralleling creek on old vehicleway. (Elevation 6,070').	2.09
0.18	Top of rise. Descend briefly.	1.91
0.19	On bank above Verde River.	1.90
0.28	Dip; aqueduct pipeline exposed on L.	1.81
0.35	Start steady ascent; pipeline on L.	1.74
0.40	Ease grade of ascent.	1.69
0.46	High above Verde River.	1.63
0.76	**Junction:** join powerline and service road from L, at small creek crossing.	1.30
0.80	Top of rise. Descend gradually, then level out.	1.29
0.96	Old ruined rock shelter above on L.	1.13
1.02	**Junction:** wider trail descends on R (no sign). Keep straight on narrow trail.	1.07
1.06	**Junction:** alternate trail on R.	1.03
1.10	**Junction:** alternate trail rejoins from R.	0.99
1.11	Top of rise.	0.98
1.14	Start steep ascent.	0.95
1.18	Level area. Rim above on R.	0.91
1.33	Top of rise.	0.76
1.36	Level section.	0.73
1.38	Start ascent.	0.71
1.48	**Important junction:** leave power line, crossing E Verde River (usually dry here) and ascending on narrow trail into forest.	0.61
1.51	Remains of rock shelter on R.	0.58
1.56	Ascend steadily.	0.53
1.57	Switchback to L, then to R in 100'. Ease grade of ascent.	0.52
1.61	Top of rise. Descend briefly, then go up again.	0.48
1.66	**Junction:** at switchback to L, Railroad Tunnel Trail [390] heads R (0.18 mi, steep ascent).	0.43
1.71	Views open to Mazatzals to S. Come around into valley, with a steady, rocky climb.	0.38
1.77	Ease briefly.	0.32
1.82	Nice section on rock shelf with cliff above to R.	0.27
1.97	Rejoin power line.	0.12
1.98	Trail signs. Go L. In 40' rejoin power line trail. Ascend steadily up rocky trail.	0.11
2.01	Ease grade of ascent.	0.08
2.08	Trail sign.	0.01
2.09	Rim Road [300] at road junction at Coconino National Forest Boundary. General Crook Trail (here a rough road) angles off sharp R. Straight ahead is Arizona Trail (dirt road) to General Springs Cabin. Elevation 7,250'.	0.00

[390] Railroad Tunnel Trail

Introduction. In 1883 there was a scheme by Chicago entrepreneur James Eddy to build the "Arizona Mineral Belt Railroad" from Phoenix to Flagstaff. A crew of 40 worked for about a month and drilled 70' of tunnel; this is where the proposed crossing of the Rim was to start. The company soon went bankrupt and that was the end of the work.

Maps. *Our Map 8 (Highline 8: RR Tunnel).* The USGS 1:24,000 Dane Canyon quadrangle (1972) shows the location of the tunnel, but not the trail.

Access. From the Col. Devin Trail [290] at 1.7 miles, or by descending on the same trail from the Rim Road [FR 300] for 0.4 mile. The trail heads east from a switchback.

General Description. This trail climbs steadily, then steeply up the side of a canyon, crossing over to the flat area at the mouth of the tunnel. The tunnel itself is not very deep. One can only imagine how difficult it would have been to build trestles to approach this area, and transport blasting material! Total elevation gain is 150'.

Read Down ↓	Detailed Trail Description	Read Up ↑
0.00	From the Col. Devin Trail head E at a sign, entering forest (6,880').	0.18
0.09	Switchback to R, then bear L.	0.09
0.12	Start steep ascent. Use care.	0.06
0.14	Ease.	0.04
0.16	Cross canyon.	0.02
0.18	Tunnel mouth and rock shelter (7,020'). W of tunnel is a narrow, non-system trail leading to an excellent view of the Mazatzals.	0.00

[30] Myrtle Trail SOUTH to NORTH

Introduction. The area of the Dude Fire is largely denuded of topsoil and live trees. This old trail, built on a good grade, has suffered from erosion and now has several severe blowdown areas. (Travel through these areas is much more tedious than the elevation and distance would seem to indicate.) Until restoration work is done, this trail is not suitable for horses.

Maps. *Our Map 10 (Highline 10: Ellison Creek).* The USGS 1:24,000 Dane Canyon quadrangle (1972) covers the approach and the trail.

Access. *At the southern end,* from the Highline Trail [31]. *At the northern end,* from FR 300 (Rim Road) at a sign, 18.1 miles east of its junction with SR 87, and 23.2 miles west of SR 260.

General Description. The trail leaves the Highline Trail where it crosses a small ridge and ascends relentlessly north. (There is not a single brief level stretch.) There are several switchbacks, but generally the trail follows the east side of the ridge that projects off the Rim to 1.1 miles, then ascends gradually to meet the Rim Road [FR 300] at 1.4 miles. Ascent is 1,040'.

Read Down ↑	Detailed Trail and Road Description	Read Up ↓
0.00	From the junction with the Highline Trail [31], ascend gradually up the ridge. Elevation 6,800' [GPS 0483480/3805800].	1.36
0.17	Drop to L of crest (blowdowns).	1.19
0.22	Use care finding trail.	1.14
0.25	Bad blowdown area.	1.11
0.27	Small dip to L. Ascend steadily NW toward ridge.	1.09
0.29	Severe blowdown area.	1.07
0.33	Use caution locating route. Follow occasional cairns.	1.03
0.36	Side-hill, again using care, ascending steeply W.	1.00
0.41	Ascend N.	0.95
0.43	**Important** switchback to L (SW). (7,090').	0.93
0.49	Very large blowdown. In 30', switchback to R.	0.87
0.51	Detour around blowdown area.	0.85
0.57	Huge blowdown (7,240').	0.79
0.76	Switchback to L near top of crest (7,430'). Use care with route here, especially on descent (as ridge is descended onto flat, do not proceed ahead, instead turn L (NE)).	0.60
0.79	Ascend steadily NNW toward rocks, then switchback R (NE) on rocks.	0.57
0.83	Side-hill just below rocks.	0.53
0.89	Sag in crest is just 35' to L. Continue up E side of crest.	0.47
1.01	Bear slightly R.	0.35
1.02	Switchback to L, in 75' to R.	0.34
1.11	Switchback to L on edge of Rim (7,740'). [GPS 0483750/3806705]....................	0.25
1.13	Cross remains of barbed-wire fence.	0.23
1.20	Excellent viewpoint 50' to L (7,820'). Follow along edge of Rim, ascending gradually. Follow cairns in open area.	0.16
1.27	Top of rise.	0.09
1.34	Top of rise. Descend with road ahead.	0.02
1.36	FR 300. Elevation 7,824'	0.00

[143] Babe Haught Trail SOUTH to NORTH

FR 289 near Tonto Fish Hatchery to FR 300

Introduction. Babe Haught was a companion of Zane Grey, the famous Western writer who lived in the area.

Maps. *Our Map 12 (Highline 12: Tonto Fish Hatchery).* The USGS 1:24,000 Knoll Lake quadrangle (1972) covers the approach but does not show the trail.

Access. *At the southern end,* from just past the Highline Trail [31] parking area, across the bridge on the Hatchery Road. This is 4 miles north of SR 260 [may change slightly with highway realignment]. *At the northern end,* from the Rim Road [FR 300], 17.4 mi west of SR 260, 23.9 miles east of SR 87.

General Description. This trail was in bad shape due to the effects of the Dude Fire. There is more erosion and brush than might be expected. In 1995 part of the mid-section was re-done. Total elevation gain is 1,400'.

Read Down ↓	Detailed Trail Description	Read Up ↑
0.00	FR 289 just north of the Fish Hatchery road. Elevation here is 6,160'. Take trail at sign, just beyond creek. Parallel creek.	2.58
0.20	Leave valley bottom, turn R, starting ascent to E. Turn R again in 15'.	2.38
0.27	Turn L.	2.31
0.29	Switchback to L, R, L again; continue zigzagging ascent.	2.29
0.46	Top of rise, on crest of spur.	2.12
0.51	**Junction:** trail of use on L. Level trail.	2.07
0.52	Start steady ascent (6,500').	2.06
0.54	Ease ascent.	2.04
0.57	Start steep ascent.	2.01
0.60	Side-hill around end of spur.	1.98
0.71	Switchback to L.	1.87
0.74	Top of rise.	1.84
0.85	Switchback to L. Ascend steeply up side of spur.	1.73
0.91	Switchback to R. 12 switchbacks continue above.	1.67
1.09	Rock slide from above. USE CARE over boulders; more damage here is likely to occur.	1.49
1.39	**Junction:** where trail goes R up narrow crest, L is viewpoint in 60'.	1.19
1.43	Crest broadens.	1.15
1.57	Top of spur ridge at edge of Rim (7,440'), fine views. Ascend gradually.	1.01
1.90	Cross small wash.	0.68
1.98	Cross small wash.	0.60
2.08	End of burn.	0.50
2.38	**Junction:** vehicleway crosses.	0.20
2.41	Top of rise. Head NE. There is no very defined way - use care.	0.17
2.58	FR 300 [Rim Road], sign (7,560').	0.00

[285] Horton Creek Trail   WEST to EAST

Introduction. One of the most popular and attractive trails in the Payson Forest District, this trail leads up a beautiful valley with a scenic creek. There are no distant views.

Maps. *Our Maps 13 & 14 (Highline 13: Horton Creek, and Highline 14: Promontory Butte).* The USGS 1:24,000 Promontory Butte quadrangle (1973) shows most of the trail accurately, but the start has changed slightly, and the last half mile is on a completely different location.

Access. *At the western end,* from FR 289, the Tonto Creek Road. Park in the obvious signed lot just west of the bridge over Tonto Creek at 0.75 mile (Horton Picnic Site). Walk back over the bridge, then take the branch road left, uphill. Reach a gate at 320', then the trailhead and register at 570' (0.1 mile). *At the eastern end,* from the Highline Trail [31].

General Description. From the Upper Tonto Campground, the trail (a former vehicleway) leads up the west side of the creek with access to falls at several places. Grades are variable but generally not steep. There are fine camping and picnic spots. At 3 miles the trail switchbacks left, then right, climbing high above a branch of Horton Creek. The Highline Trail is reached at 3.4 miles. Total elevation gain is 1,250'.

Cautions. The footway is rocky in places and can be muddy after wet weather. In places the creek has undercut the banks and caution must be used.

Read Down ↓	Detailed Trail Description	Read Up ↑
0.00	From trailhead sign and register on campground road, descend NE. Reach bottom in 140' and parallel creek. Elevation 5,450'.	3.38
0.05	Cross creek (often dry here). Immediately start ascent above creek.	3.33
0.11	Gate in barbed-wire fence.	3.27
0.43	**Junction:** on R trail of use leads along creek bank and thru possible camping areas. Keep L on rockier, wider trail ascending.	2.95
0.46	Hiker's gate in barbed-wire fence.	2.92
0.90	On R, falls on the creek are worth exploring.	2.48
0.94	**Junction:** sharp R leads back to creek. Continue ascent.	2.46
1.14	Top of rise (5,780'). Descend briefly to NE, then ascend.	2.24
1.16	Bottom of descent; bear L.	2.22
1.35	**Junction:** trail of use sharp R.	2.03
1.39	Landmark: go between cut end of log and rock.	1.99
1.43	Ascend steadily on rocky trail, keep to L.	1.95
1.53	**Junction:** trail spur to R leads 350' to bench above creek, then trails descend L & R to creek. This is a very beautiful area.	1.85
1.62	Top of rise. Descend gradually to N.	1.76
1.65	Cross wash from L; trail of use on R. Ascend steadily to NE (5,880').	1.73
1.69	Top of rise. Less rocky.	1.69
1.72	Top of rise.	1.66
1.74	**Junction:** alternate trail re-enters on R.	1.64
1.77	Bottom of descent.	1.61

1.79	**Junction:** trail R leads 100' to falls on creek, another fine area.	1.59
1.83.	Open area.	1.55
1.94	Eroded bank just above creek.	1.44
2.04	**Junction:** trail R leads 50' to falls over rock shelf.	1.34
2.09	Start ascent.	1.29
2.15	Attractive area with falls on creek.	1.23
2.16	Top of rise.	1.22
2.20	**Junction:** trail R leads 40' to upper end of slick-rock area of creek. Ascend steadily.	1.18
2.31	Ascend rocky stretch.	1.07
2.35	Views over creek. Continue steady ascent.	1.03
2.40	Top of rise.	0.98
2.49	Big rock field on R. Ascend very steadily N.	0.89
2.55	Wash on L; rocky ascent.	0.83
2.86	**Junction:** trail R leads 150' to creek, slick-rock area and deep pool. Switchback to L, then swing R.	0.52
3.38	**Junction:** Highline Trail [31]. Elevation 6,680'.	0.00

To the right along the Highline Trail east, the sign pointing to the Horton Spring Trail [292] to the Rim is in the wrong location (or should have an arrow pointing to the east). The trail junction is 180' further along (ascends a small ridge to the north with no sign, and the spring is up this trail). Continuing, 40' further is a barbed-wire fence and 35' more brings one to the crossing of Horton Creek below the spring.

[292] Horton Springs Trail SOUTH to NORTH

Horton Springs to FR 300

Introduction. One of the steepest, roughest trails up the Rim, the Horton Springs Trail is not recommended for casual use, but can be used as part of long circuit trips including the Babe Haught Trail [143] and Highline Trail to the west, or the See Canyon Trail [184] and Highline Trail to the east.

Maps. *Our Map 14 (Highline 14: Promontory Butte).* The USGS 1:24,000 quadrangles Promontory Butte (1973) and Knoll Lake (1972) do not show the trail.

Access. *At the southern end,* from the Highline Trail [31] 3.4 miles east of FR 289, or 3.4 miles north of Tonto Campground via the Horton Creek Trail. Head up the crestline of the spur obvious from the gate on the side-trail to the Springs. (NOTE: this is *not* from the trail signpost near the junction with the Horton Creek Trail, 225' further west.) *At the northern end,* from FR 300 [Rim Road] 14.7 miles west of SR 260, and 26.6 miles east of SR 87.

General Description. This trail switchbacks up a ridge relentlessly, with fine views, but lots of exposure. *It is not advisable to take this trail in bad weather.* There are some blow-downs and the slope is very steep. FR 300 is reached at 1.25 miles. It is recommended for the ascent rather than the descent. Total elevation gain is 1,240'.

Read Down ↓	Detailed Trail Description	Read Up ↑
0.00	From just W of where the outlet of Horton Springs crosses, follow trail N. *NOTE:* This is a very confusing area, heavily used by campers, with many trails of use. *Follow these directions closely.* Elevation is 6,640'. In 55' switchback to R and ascend, then turn L, easing ascent at 125'. At 180' pass through camping areas, heading NE. At 250' turn R, toward gate in barbed-wire fence.	1.23
0.06	**Junction:** at gate in fence, a constructed trail switchbacks down 165' to beautiful Horton Spring, gushing from the hillside. *Do not go thru fence;* instead turn L, following fence line steeply uphill. Soon you will see cairns.	1.17
0.09	Switchback to R, then turn L in 25'.	1.14
0.11	Ease grade of ascent.	1.12
0.14	Ascend steeply up rocks.	1.09
0.17	Switchback to L, continue steep ascent.	1.06
0.44	Turn R up exposed crest (dangerous in bad weather). Elevation 7,160'.	0.78
0.70	Switchback to L, then to R in 15'.	0.53
0.71	Cross over crest to opposite (W) side (7,540').	0.52
0.79	Switchback to L just before crest, then to R in 115'.	0.44
0.81	Switchback to R (7,670'), then to L in 50'.	0.42
0.83	Blow-down area. *USE CARE WITH ROUTE-FINDING HERE.*	0.40
0.97	Ascend near rim edge (7,820').	0.26
1.03	Top of rise (7,840').	0.20
1.12	Bottom of descent; seep.	0.11
1.21	Top of rise.	0.02
1.23	This trail ends at FR 300 [Rim Road], elevation 7,880'.	0.00

[33] Derrick Trail WEST to EAST

Introduction. For a good walk in open forest, this gradual ascent up a long ridge is ideal.

Maps. *Our Maps 13 & 14 (Highline 13: Horton Creek, and Highline 14: Promontory Butte).* The USGS 1:24,000 Promontory Butte quadrangle (1973) shows the trail, but its end at the intersection with the Highline Trail is now at a different location, about 0.6 mile southwest of the junction shown on the topoographic map. This accounts for the shorter trail distance than on the old trail signs. Its intersection with the Derrick Spur Trail [32] is also altered.

Access. *At the western end,* from the Upper Tonto Creek Campground Road, 740' from FR 289. FR 289 is 22.9 miles east of Payson. *At the eastern end,* from the Highline Trail [31], 3 miles east of Horton Springs and 4.4 miles west of FR 284.

General Description. This trail has a reasonable grade all the way to the Highline Trail. The lower mile is fine walking, but then it becomes rockier, with some trenching from poor drainage and heavy past usage. At 0.6 mile it meets the Derrick Spur Trail [32] ascending from FR 289, which can be used for a circuit trip. There are only a few views, and those are limited. Total ascent is 900'.

Read Down ↓	Detailed Trail Description	Read Up ↑
0.00	From the campground road to "Units 7, 8, 9", trail starts climbing NE (5,500').	2.20
0.03	Switchback to R (S).	2.17
0.11	**Junction:** old vehicleway ascends to L. Continue ascent on fine trail.	2.09
0.18	**Junction:** old vehicleway enters from L at barbed-wire fence. Sign indicates trail maintenance by Boy Scout Troop #75 under the Adopt-a-Trail Program.	2.02
0.38	Ease grade of ascent.	1.82
0.43	Head ESE, descend briefly, then continue up in 120'.	1.77
0.48	**Junction:** keep R where old trail heads to L.	1.72
0.53	**Junction:** rejoins.	1.67
0.59	**Important junction:** Derrick Spur Trail [32] goes up-hill on R (0.86 mi to FR 289 near SR 260). Elevation 5,770'. Ascend old eroded trail route.	1.61
0.66	**Junction:** with old trail ahead destroyed by severe slumping, go R & up.	1.54
0.74	**Junction:** return to old route.	1.46
0.80	**Junction:** depart from old route on R; wind along top of broad crest.	1.40
1.36	Ascend steadily thru semi-open, rocky area.	0.84
1.94	Rocky, trenched trailway.	0.26
2.10	Top of rise (6,420'). Descend along barbed-wire fence.	0.10
2.20	**Junction:** Highline Trail [31] West is straight ahead; East is to the R. Horton Spring is 3 mi; elevation here is 6,400'.	0.00

[32] Derrick Spur Trail   WEST to EAST

Introduction. A short alternate to the Derrick Trail, especially from the Lower Tonto Campground area, can make an interesting loop trip.

Maps. *Our Map 13 (Highline 13: Horton Creek).* The USGS 1:24,000 Promontory Butte quadrangle (1973, airphotos 1965) shows this trail in the correct location except for its connection with the Derrick Trail [33] (it actually drops down from the crest).

Access. *At the western end,* from FR 289 (Tonto Creek) just past the cattleguard where the road starts from SR 260. This is 22.9 miles east of the crossroads in Payson. The trail is visible entering the forest through a gate in the barbed-wire fence. (This approach may be slightly altered due to the 4-laning of SR 260 in 2004.) *At the eastern end,* from the Derrick Trail [33], 0.6 mile above Upper Tonto Campground.

General Description. This trail switchbacks up a spur to its top at 0.6 mile, then follows the crest of the spur, dropping to the Derrick Trail [33] at 0.9 mile. It is less used than the Derrick Trail, and is somewhat noisy from the traffic on SR 260. Total ascent is 400'.

Read Down ↓	Detailed Trail Description	Read Up ↑
0.00	From cattleguard near where FR 289 leaves SR 260, trail starts into forest at sign (elevation 5,410').	0.87
0.01	Pass thru gate in barbed-wire fence, then turn L along fence line.	0.86
0.07	Sign indicating that this trail is maintained by the Payson Lions under the Adopt-a-Trail Program.	0.80
0.13	Turn R, away from fence, and ascend steadily N.	0.74
0.16	Pass under power line.	0.71
0.20	Switchback to L.	0.67
0.23	Switchback to R (long traverse).	0.64
0.33	Switchback to L.	0.54
0.37	Switchback to R.	0.50
0.41	Switchback to L, then to R in 140'.	0.46
0.46	Switchback to L.	0.41
0.49	Turn R (some views here).	0.38
0.64	Top of rise.	0.23
0.68	Descend to N.	0.19
0.71	Top of rise (5,810'). Turn L, descend.	0.16
0.77	Top of rise (5,800'). Descend steadily.	0.10
0.87	**Junction:** Derrick Trail [33] L & R (elevation 5,770'.	0.00

[184] See Canyon Trail SOUTH to NORTH

Introduction. This is one of the more varied and sheltered ways up the Rim. The See Spring Trail [185] is a short side-trail to a good spring.

Maps. *Our Map 15 (Highline 15: See Canyon).* The USGS 1:24,000 Promontory Butte quadrangle (1973) shows the original trail, but there have changes in location since then.

Access. *At the southern end,* from See Canyon Trailhead at end of FR 284, 1.7 miles from SR 260 in Christopher Creek. *At the northern end*, from FR 300 (Rim Road), 29.8 miles east of SR 87, or 11.5 miles west of SR 260.

General Description. This trail leaves the trailhead area, diverges from the Highline Trail and passes a junction with the See Spring Trail [185] at 0.7 mile. It crosses Christopher Creek at 1.1 miles and ascends high above it. As it ascends more steeply, it will cross it 4 more times. In the last half mile it climbs out of the valley to the Rim at 3.6 miles. (Note: the start goes through a confusing area criss-crossed with trails.) Total ascent is 1,750'.

Read Down ↓	Detailed Trail Description	Read Up ↑
0.00	From See Canyon Trailhead (elevation 6,160'), head SE at trailhead sign, descending.	3.55
0.03	**Junction:** join Highline Trail [31] and turn L (downhill) on it.	3.52
0.05	**Junction (4-way):** where trails of use go up and downstream, cross Christopher Creek (use care in times of high water). Ascend steep bank.	3.50
0.07	On top of bank. Picnic area to L. Keep R.	3.48
0.14	**Important junction:** where Highline Trail turns R, go straight (sign), rising gradually.	3.41
0.28	**Junction:** trail of use to L crosses creek and leads back to trailhead in 0.14 mi.	3.27
0.25	**Junction:** trail of use on L to area used for camping. Bear R.	3.16
0.68	**Junction:** See Spring Trail [185] goes R here (sign). Elev. 6,340'.	2.87
0.75	Cross major side-creek (from See Spring).	2.80
0.81	Cross seep.	2.74
0.83	Cross seep.	2.72
0.99	Turn R.	2.69
1.10	Cross dry side-creek.	2.58
1.14	Cross Christopher Creek.	2.41
1.19	Ascend steadily high above ChristopherCreek.	2.36
1.28	Top of rise.	2.27
1.53	Switchback L, then R.	2.02
1.61	Descend bank.	1.94
1.63	Bottom of descent.	1.92
1.72	Switchback to L, then to R in 40'.	1.83
1.76	Descend bank.	1.79
1.78	Switchback R.	1.77
1.80	Cross Christopher Creek (6,650'). Ascend opposite bank.	1.75
1.92	Switchback to R, rising steeply, high above creek.	1.63
1.96	Slump - CAUTION! You can go above it on narrow trail.	1.59
2.08	Turn L, cross Christopher Creek. Use care on boulders; follow cairns.	1.47
2.10	Other side of creek. Ascend a very steep stretch. In 80' turn R.	1.45

2.17	Cross Christopher Creek (6,810'). Use care. On other side, side-hill steep bank.	1.38
2.39	Landmark: go between cut log ends. Parallel creek on R.	1.16
2.56	Switchback to R (7,160'). Ascend steeply.	0.99
2.58	Top of rise. In 55' a side-wash is crossed. Trail is very steep in sections.	0.97
2.68	Switchback to L. Rock outcrop above to R. Ascend steeply W, then SW.	0.87
2.71	Switchback to R, then to L in 40' with a very steep pitch.	0.84
2.73	Switchback R. Landmark: in 45' go around end of big blowdown. Side-hill on beautiful trail.	0.82
2.79	Top of rise.	0.76
2.84	Cross side-creek and sag.	0.71
2.87	Top of rise.	0.68
2.97	Cross Christopher Creek, here small. Parallel it on L.	0.58
3.06	Cross Christopher Creek (7,470').	0.49
3.11	Cross creek to R in a beautiful area.	0.44
3.25	Switchback to L.	0.30
3.26	Turn R and ascend steep pitch on rocky bank above creek.	0.29
3.38	Bear L, ascend steep, rocky pitch.	0.17
3.42	Top of rise.	0.13
3.51	Cross old vehicleway near fire ring.	0.04
3.55	**Junction:** FR 300 on Rim, elevation 7,860'.	0.00

[185] See Spring Trail

Introduction. This short side-trail leads to a permanent spring.

Maps. *Our Map 15 (See Canyon).* The USGS 1:24,000 Promotory Butte quadrangle (1973) covers the approach but does not show the trail.

Access. From 0.68 mile on the See Canyon Trail [184].

General Description. From the east bank of Christopher Creek this trail leads up a small valley, crosses the creek that issues from See Spring, and enters a camping area before reaching the Spring at 0.6 mile. Total ascent is 300'.

Read Down ↓	Detailed Trail Description	Read Up ↑
0.00	From See Canyon Trail [185] at 0.68 mi, go R (elevation 6,340').	0.62
0.20	Viewpoint over creek.	0.42
0.31	Head up bank of side-creek.	0.31
0.32	Slumping bank.	0.30
0.34	Start steep ascent (short pitch).	0.28
0.38	Slumping bank.	0.24
0.41	Slumping bank. Use care.	0.21
0.46	Cross creek, use care. Trail is less obvious from here.	0.16
0.58	Camping area on R.	0.04
0.62	Trail ends at spring (elevation 6,640').	0.00

[296] Pump Station Trail   SOUTH to NORTH

FR 32A to Highline Trail [31]

Maps. *Our Map 7 (Highline 7: Washington Park).* The USGS 1:24,000 Kehl Ridge quadrangle (1972) covers none of the route of this trail.

Access. *At the southern end,* from the pump station just east of where FR 32A turns north. *At the northern end,* from the Highline Trail [31] 0.25 mile east of Washington Park Trailhead.

General Description. The trail is not used often, and in places is confused with trails of use. It starts at the pump station just past where FR 32A turns north. It crosses Christopher Creek and heads upstream. After a quarter of a mile, it ascends the hillside and side-hills a low ridge, reaching the Highline Trail at 0.9 mile. Ascent is 300'.

Read Down ↓	Detailed Trail Description	Read Up ↑
0.00	From road off FR 32A at pump station (5,780'), cross creek.	0.92
0.05	**Junction:** another approach on L, with log across creek.	0.87
0.28	Leave almost level area, ascend.	0.64
0.30	Turn L.	0.62
0.47	Top of rise.	0.45
0.56	Cross sag.	0.36
0.58	Cross sag.	0.34
0.64	On flat rocks, watch carefully for trail.	0.28
0.68	Huge boulder on R.	0.24
0.69	Top of rise.	0.23
0.72	Above river.	0.20
0.84	Sag.	0.08
0.92	Highline Trail [31] 0.23 mi E of Washington Park TH. Elevation 6,040'.	0.00

[291] Drew Trail SOUTH to NORTH

Introduction. A steep but graded trail (may not be suitable for horses) leads up the Rim from the Highline Trail, offering some good views. It was an old pioneer trail, built before 1909, the name reflecting the Drew family whose homestead was in the area. A circuit trip can be made using this trail, a section of the Rim Road [FR 300], the See Canyon Trail [184], and the Highline Trail.

Maps. *Our Map 16 (Drew Trail).* The USGS 1:24,000 Woods Canyon quadrangle (Provisional, 1990) accurately shows the location of the trail.

Access. *At the southern end,* from the Highline Trail [31], 4.1 miles west of Two-Sixty Trailhead. *At the northern end,* from FR 9350, 0.8 mile off the Rim Road [300], at a point 5.2 miles west of SR 260.

General Description. This trail switchbacks up the steep side of the Rim for 1/3 mile, then has a few brief respites before beginning a steady 0.25-mile climb at 0.6 mile. From 0.9 mile the trail is at a somewhat easier grade to 1.1 miles, where it ends. Total elevation gain is 840'.

Read Down ↓	Detailed Trail Description	Read Up ↑
0.00	From the Highline Trail 4.1 mi W of 260 TH, head uphill (6,790').	1.08
0.05	Switchback to L.	1.03
0.13	Switchback to L again.	0.95
0.15	**Junction:** avoid trail of use straight ahead; switchback to R.	0.93
0.17	Switchback to L, then to R in 30', where at a **junction**, avoid trail of use on L.	0.91
0.20	Top of rise.	0.88
0.33	Top of rise.	0.75
0.34	Bottom of brief descent. Ascend steeply.	0.74
0.43	Top of rise. Brief level area.	0.65
0.47	Top of rise (7,170').	0.61
0.53	Level stretch.	0.55
0.56	Cross (often dry) creek (7,210'), ascend.	0.52
0.58	Minor sag. Start very steady, rocky ascent [Use special care on descent].	0.50
0.86	Major switchback to L. Grade eases.	0.22
1.05	Fence posts from former gate, no sign.	0.03
1.08	FR 9350 just back from edge of Rim (7,590').	0.00

[179] Military Sinkhole Trail EAST to WEST

Introduction. This area was on the route of General George Crook's military road between Fort Verde and Fort McDowell. In June-July of 2002 a devastating wildfire consumed over 450,000 acres just east of here in the largest fire in Arizona history, the 'Rodeo-Chediski' Fire.[1]

Maps. *Our Map 17 (Highline 17: 260 Trailhead).* The USGS 1:24,000 Woods Canyon quadrangle (Provisional Edition, 1990) covers the approach and the trail, but shows its western alignment incorrectly.

Access. *At the eastern end,* from 1.9 miles on FR 300, just north of where SR 260 hits the Rim. The sign indicates "Rim Vista Lakes Trail" at the start. *At the western end,* from Two-Sixty Trailhead, 24 miles east of Payson. [This distance will be slightly changed by the new highway alignment.]

General Description. A rapid 700' drop off the Rim onto an old vehicleway for a mile leads to an up-and-down section along the flank of the Rim. Many creek valleys are crossed. At 2.4 miles the Two-Sixty Trailhead is reached, where the Highline Trail starts westward. Total descent is about 1,000'.

Read Down ↓	Detailed Trail Description	Read Up ↑
0.00	From FR 300 (elev. 7,600'), take the Rim Vista Trail W for 320' to a **junction** and start of this trail, which descends rapidly with occasional views.	2.35
0.26	Ease grade of descent.	2.09
0.28	Bottom of descent. Level briefly.	2.07
0.39	Cross small creek (7,300').	1.96
0.69	Views on R (SE) (7,120'). Descend rocky stretch.	1.66
0.91	Swing R (SE), ease.	1.44
0.95	**Junction:** leave old vehicleway on R, taking trail that ascends (6,900'). Go up & down.	1.40
1.08	Ascend steadily.	1.27
1.10	Cross creek valley. Bear L, ascend steeply.	1.25
1.11	Top of rise (6,930'). Descend to W, then to NE.	1.24
1.18	Top of rise.	1.17
1.23	Bottom of descent in draw.	1.12
1.27	Top of rise; descend W.	1.08
1.31	Cross small sag, then others in 70' and 105'.	1.04
1.58	Bottom of descent.	0.77
1.66	Descend into canyon (6,900').	0.69
1.68	Cross creek, head NW.	0.67
1.75	Cross small creek.	0.60
1.79	Bottom of descent. [There may be a blow-down area here.]	0.56
1.81	Cross large, scoured creek, ascend to S.	0.54
1.83	Top of rise; descend.	0.52
1.88	Sag with small creek.	0.47
2.06	Small sag.	0.29
2.08	Turn R.	0.27
2.09	Switchback to L.	0.26

---

[1]According to the news reports, these fires were set by two misguided people, one a lost white hiker to get attention, and the other by a part-time Apache firefighter.

2.10	Cross creek.	0.25
2.15	Open, rocky area with some views.	0.20
2.28	Turn L (SE), descend.	0.07
2.35	**Junction:** Two-Sixty Trailhead, corral, toilet; elevation 6,660'. The Highline Trail [31] starts here, heading W.	0.00

At the upper end, on the opposite side of FR 300, the trail continues north-ward, following metal markers, descends at 115', and reaches the bottom next to the Sinkhole at 300'. A pond is on the left. At 0.2 mile it turns right and ascends for 185', reaching the top in a semi-open area. A dirt road is crossed at 0.4 mile and the trail ends at 0.44 mile at the General Crook Trail markers (chevrons).

Rim Road [FR 300] Mileage Summary

38.1 miles unpaved, about 3 hours

Mileage W→E Read Down	Reference Point	Mileage E→W Read Up
0.0	**SR 87, 2.8 mi E of junction with SR 260**	41.3
0.1	FR 218A on R to Milk Ranch Point, turn L	41.2
1.3	Track R to lookout tower	40.0
3.4	Fr 218 on R, FR 147 L	37.9
5.3	FR 308 on L	36.0
6.5	Kehl Spring on L & CG	34.8
7.0	FR 141 on L	34.3
8.2	Hi-View Point on R	33.1
8.7	FR 320 on L	32.6
9.8	FR 501 on L	31.5
10.6	FR 123 on L	30.7
11.4	Battle of Big Dry Wash marker; trail [290] on R; to General Springs Cabin on L [AZ Trail X]	29.9
12.1	FR 393 on L	29.2
12.4	FR 95 on L	28.9
12.5	FR 398 on L	28.8
13.9	Dude Lake on L	27.4
15.3	Trail [171] on L (Coconino NF)	26.0
15.5	FR 139 on L	25.8
16.9	FR 145 on L	24.4
17.7	FR 321 on L, rough section after	23.6
18.1	Myrtle Trail [30] on R	23.2
19.2	FR 137 on L	22.1
20.9	FR 300H on L	20.4
21.9	FR 295E on L	19.4
23.9	Babe Haught Trail [143] on R	17.4
24.3	Enter Apache-Sitgreaves NF	17.0
25.7	FR 115 on L	15.6
26.6	Horton Springs Trail [292] on R	14.7
29.0	FR 215 on L	12.3
29.3	FR 89 on L	12.0
29.4	FR 76 on R	11.9
29.8	See Canyon Trail [184] on R	11.5
30.2	FR 208 on L	11.1

30.3	Promontory Lookout on L	11.0
30.9	FR 84 on L	10.4
31.5	FR 9354 on R	9.8
32.1	FR 34 ahead	9.2
32.4	FR 169 on L	8.9
35.8	FR 195 on L to camping area	5.5
36.1	FR 9350 on R to camping area & Drew Trail [291	5.2
37.5	Mogollon CG on R	3.8
38.1	**Paving starts**; L to Woods Canyon Lake	3.2
38.2	Parking on R for Rim Lakes Vista Trail [622]	3.1
38.6	Parking on R for Rim Vista Trail	2.7
39.4	Military Sinkhole Tr [179] parking & viewpoint on R	1.9
40.7	Rim CG on R	0.6
41.2	Rimtop TH on L	0.1
41.3	**SR 260, Rim Visitor Center**	0.0

Other Payson

Area Trails

[251] Walnut Trail NORTH to SOUTH

[Part of Arizona Trail]

Introduction. The trails in this area have been redesignated recently. The short section from trail [16] to the start of trail [251] is part of the Arizona Trail.

Maps. *Our Map 19 (AZ Trail East: Pine/Strawberry).* The USGS 1:24,000 quadrangles Buckhead Mesa (1973) and Cane Springs Mountain (1967) cover part of the jeep trail and power line sections only.

Access. *At the northern end,* from FR 428, 2 miles west of SR 87; at the southern end, from the end of trail [540], a jeep road serving Point Tank, 3.8 miles from FR 194.

General Description. This trail descends to a side-trail junction, then briefly rises over a height of land, then follows Oak Spring Canyon, re-crossing it multiple times, to a junction with the Oak Spring (Arizona) Trail [16] at 1.7 miles. From here it ascends steadily up the side of a broad ridge, to Ridge Tank at 2.7 miles, ending at 3.1 miles at the start of the Power Line Trail [504]. Total ascent is 650'.

Read Down ↓	Detailed Trail Description	Read Up ↑
0.00	From FR 194 aross from the Pine-Strawberry Trail [16], head S, descending. Elevation 5,740'.	3.11
0.10	**Junction:** trail L descends [Detailed side-trail data: Go along a hogback in 250', cross small creek in 350', then reach the top of a rise at 0.2 mi. Then descend, paralleling the creek on the L. At 0.3 mi reach a junction (straight ahead leads to private land). Go L here, crossing the creek at 0.31 mi, ascending very steadily out of its valley, to reach FR 428 at 0.39 mi.]	3.01
0.13	Top of rise (5,780'). Descend gradually, following Oak Spring Canyon.	2.98
0.27	Cross side-creek.	2.84
0.34	Re-cross it.	2.77
0.45	Re-cross it.	2.66
0.49	Re-cross it.	2.62
0.52	Re-cross it.	2.59
0.54	Re-cross it.	2.57
0.57	Re-cross it.	2.54
0.59	Leave creek bed on L.	2.52
0.62	Join creek.	2.49
0.63	Level camping area.	2.48
0.65	Cross creek.	2.46
0.67	Re-cross creek.	2.44
0.68	Waterfall site on R.	2.43
0.75	Cross creek.	2.36
0.81	Level.	2.30
0.85	Top of rise.	2.26
0.87	In main creek bed. Continue along valley bottom.	2.24
1.54	Top of rise (5,370'). Descend rocky slope.	1.57
1.68	**Important junction:** Oak Spring Trail [16] on L leads 3.2 mi E to SR 87. (5,240') Continue on jeep road, ascending [now on Arizona Trail section].	1.43
2.04	Cross wash.	1.07

2.10 Ascend steadily up side of ridge above Oak Spring (on L). 1.01
2.68 Top of rise at Ridge Tank (on R). Ascent eases. 0.43
3.11 **Junction:** join jeep road (L descends to Point Tank) (5,850'). To continue, trail
      designation at this point becomes Powerline Trail [540] leading 5.72 mi to
      FR 194 on Hardscrabble Mesa. *This trail ends.* 0.00

[15] Pine-Strawberry Trail   SOUTH to NORTH

FR 428 to SR 87

Introduction. The countryside is attractive, with some varied terrain and views, but not spectacular. The trail is used mostly by equestrians.

Maps. *Our Map 19 (AZ Trail East: Pine/Strawberry).* The USGS 1:24,000 Buckhead Mesa and Pine quadrangles (1973) cover the approaches but do not show the trail.

Access. At the southern end, from FR 428 (Hardscrabble Road), 2 miles from SR 87 in Pine. At the northern end, from SR 87 half a mile east of Strawberry, at a corral and trailhead south of the highway.

General Description. For 4.25 miles it slabs the wooded side of Strawberry Mountain, passing a side-trail at 1.2 miles, then ascends a draw to reach SR 87 at a trailhead. There are few views. Ascent is 300'.

Read Down ↓	Detailed Trail Description	Read Up ↑
0.00	Leave FR 428 at sign (5,720').	4.24
0.07	Switchback to L.	4.17
0.09	Turn R.	4.15
0.19	Switchback to L.	4.05
0.23	Switchback to R.	4.01
0.97	Switchback to R, then to L in 50'.	3.27
1.15	Switchback to R.	3.09
1.18	Switchback to L.	3.06
1.20	**Junction:** trail sharp R descends, paralleling wash, to 0.26 mi, where there is a junction: straight ahead descends to 0.29 mi at FR 428 at the Tonto National Forest boundary. To the R, trail spur leads at 0.28 mi to FR 428 at road designation sign. Continue straight ahead.	3.04
1.21	Cross wash in valley.	3.03
1.68	Cross creek in valley.	2.56
1.94	Turn slightly L in flat area; to R, short spur descends to spring.	2.30
1.96	Cross wash.	2.28
2.03	Switchback to L, then to R in 250'.	2.21
2.39	Switchback sharp R, then to L in 250'.	1.85
2.90	Cross moderate wash in draw.	1.34
2.97	**Junction:** faint trail descends R.	1.27
3.54	**Junction:** sharp R, trail descends.	0.70
3.79	Enter small draw, follow it.	0.45
3.91	Follow draw again.	0.33
4.08	Follow line of cairns from here.	0.16
4.21	Trail sign, bear R.	0.03
4.24	Trail ends at fence in trailhead area. Parking area is 100' ahead, SR 87 is at 250'. Elevation 6,000'	0.00

[540] Powerline Trail SOUTH to NORTH

General Description. This is mostly a jeep or service road that provides a circuitous link in the Arizona Trail and has some views. Total elevation gain is about 700'.

Maps. *Our Maps 18 & 19 (Pine/Strawberry and Hardscrabble Mesa).* The USGS Buckhead Mesa (1973) and Cane Springs Mountain (1967) quadrangles (1:24,000) cover the terrain but only show the trail's first section.

Access. *From the south,* from the Oak Spring Trail at 1.43 miles south of the junction with trails [16] and [251]. *From the north,* from FR 194, which is 3 miles from FR 708 (Fossil Springs Road) just west of Strawberry.

Cautions. There are a number of access vehicleways that are growing in and can be confusing. Marking is minimal.

Read Down ↓	Detailed Road & Trail Description	Read Up ↑
0.00	From trail **junction** with Walnut Trail [251], 1.43 mi from junction with [16], head W on jeep road (5,850').	5.72
0.25	Cross under power line.	5.47
0.73	Top of rise (5,955'). Sign for trail [251]. Descend SW.	4.99
0.85	Gate in barbed-wire fence (open); stock tank on R. Descend.	4.87
0.88	Bottom of descent; vehicleway on L.	4.84
1.08	Open gate in barbed-wire fence.	4.64
1.40	Top of rise.	4.32
1.53	**Junction:** track on L.	4.19
1.69	Bottom of descent.	4.03
1.94	**Junction:** L to camping area.	3.78
2.00	**Junction:** keep L where vehicleway goes R.	3.72
2.07	Bottom of descent.	3.65
2.20	Top of rise.	3.52
2.53	**Junction:** keep R on descent.	3.19
2.58	**Junction:** poorer vehicleway sharp L.	3.14
2.79	**Junction:** keep L.	2.93
2.80	Go thru barbed-wire fence.	2.92
3.09	**Junction:** vehicleways L & R.	2.63
3.42	Way becomes clearer.	2.30
3.51	**Junction:** FR 1654 on R.	2.21
3.69	Cross small wash, cross under power line.	2.03
3.98	**Junction:** FR 427 R.	1.74
4.41	Gate in barbed-wire fence.	1.31
4.85	Bottom of descent.	0.87
5.15	**Junction:** old vehicleway crosses; L to tank.	0.57
5.50	Take old, faint vehicleway, L from power line.	0.22
5.72	**Junction:** FR 194, elevation 5,940'.	0.00

For Arizona Trail continuation south, head west on FR 194 for 1.4 miles to Whiterock Mesa trail [14], which leads to the East Verde River.

[18] Fossil Springs Trail SOUTH to NORTH

FR 784 to Fossil Springs

Introduction. Fossil Springs is a popular area in a beautiful riparian location with many different kinds of trees. The springs themselves are an amazing outpouring of a million gallons an hour of crystal clear (but heavily mineralized) water. The canyon itself is very attractive if the weather is not too hot.

Maps. *Our Map 20 (Fossil Creek).* The USGS 1:24,000 Strawberry quadrangle (1967) covers the approach and shows the trail.

Access. *At the southern end,* from FR 784 0.1 mile from FR 708, which is 4.7 miles from SR 87 in Strawberry (Fossil Springs Road). Road signs on FR 708 may still say "3/4 mile" for the trailhead access, which has now been shortened. Depending upon when the road was last graded, low-clearance vehicles may have difficulty with FR 784; drive with care. *At the northern end,* from the end of the Flume Trail (mostly FR 154), 4.6 miles from the trailhead at FR 708.

General Description. The trail (an old vehicleway) is maintained by the Arizona Boys Ranch and descends east on the northern face of the ridge, with fine views. At just under 1 mile two major washes are crossed and the trail then switches to a northerly and northwesterly direction. Several sections are quite rocky. At 2.75 miles is a junction where the trail to the springs turns left, crossing Fossil Creek, entering the Fossil Springs Wilderness and reaching the upper springs at 3.2 miles. Total elevation loss is 1,200'.

Read Down ↓	Detailed Trail Description	Read Up ↑
0.00	From the trailhead at 5,600', sign the register just below (check yourself back out, too). The trail (a narrow old vehicleway, rocky in spots) descends steadily to the N with fine views over the Fossil Creek valley.	3.19
0.08	Ease grade of descent.	3.11
0.34	Bear L. In 70' descend rocky trail to NNW.	2.85
0.48	Ease, head N, then E (5,420').	2.71
0.69	Turn R (SE).	2.50
0.73	Turn L & R, descending steadily.	2.46
0.77	Ease grade of descent; trailway improves.	2.42
0.78	Swing L & then R, descend steadily.	2.41
0.83	Turn R (5,310').	2.36
0.85	Turn L (wash on R); descend to N.	2.34
0.90	Turn R.	2.29
0.93	Bottom of descent. Ascend to NE.	2.26
0.95	Cross wash; swing NNW.	2.24
0.98	Cross major wash (5,260'); head SW (rocky).	2.21
1.09	Round end of small wash (5,220'). Easy descent to W.	2.10
1.19	Trail rocky again.	2.00
1.25	Top of rise; descend steeply.	1.94
1.29	Turn L (to SW).	1.90
1.31	Switchback to R.	1.88
1.35	Switchback to L.	1.84

1.41	Bear L on level trail, then ascend gradually.	1.78
1.51	Top of rise (5,120'). Descend to NW.	1.68
1.59	Flat camping area on L (old trail of use on L).	1.60
1.61	Top of rise; descend to NW.	1.58
1.80	Descend to NE on rocky trail (5,100').	1.39
1.89	**Junction:** where vehicleway continues straight ahead, turn L and descend (5,060').	1.30
2.00	Descend steadily.	1.19
2.12	Top of rise (4,890'). Descend to W, then rockily to NW.	1.07
2.65	Gate in barbed-wire fence.	0.54
2.67	Descend rocky trail.	0.52
2.75	**Important junction:** trail R leads 0.38 mi to Wilderness Boundary, and beyond to the Mail Trail [84], some 3 mi in the Coconino National Forest, to the N Rim and 4WD road. Trail to L is the extension of the Mail Trail to Fossil Springs, partly in... Coconino National Forest; take it. (Elevation 4,480'.).	0.44
2.82	Descend rocky trail.	0.37
2.89	**Junction:** trail of use to creek on R.	0.30
2.95	Cross boulders of Fossil Creek (often dry). Ascend opposite bank.	0.24
2.96	Top of rise. Cross Fossil Creek Wilderness Boundary. Pleasant area.	0.23
3.02	**Junction:** trail of use to L leads to Fossil Creek in 130'.	0.17
3.11	**Important junction:** where Flume Trail continues S (uphill) & W toward the dam and flume, go L on well-worn side-trail.	0.08
3.15	At edge of spring area, one can go R (along ledge) or L across roots and boulders.	0.04
3.19	Fossil Springs gushes out of the ground at an impressive volume. (A large shaded pool invites some to swim here.) Elevation 4,400'.	0.00

There are better camping areas further along Fossil Creek between 0.1 and 0.4 mile on the Flume Trail. By the Flume Trail it is 4.6 miles to Flume Trail-head at FR 708. The fate of the Flume Trail on the service road, and of the flume itself, are discussed in the section on it.

[FR 154] Flume Trail WEST to EAST

From FR 708 to Fossil Springs

Introduction. Fossil Springs is a popular area in a beautiful riparian location. The springs themselves are an amazing outpouring of crystal clear water. The Irving Power Plant at the start of this trail is being decommissioned[1] along with the Childs Power Plant at the Verde River at the end of 2004 (at present the turn-of-the-century flume is still being used). This will result in a return of the water to the creek bed and probably a greatly increased public use of the area, perhaps with new facilities (at the time of publication, it was expected that the flume will be removed and the service road turned into a trail for day use only). This description will probably remain accurate for the next few years, but if in doubt, check with the Forest Service office.

Maps. *Our Map 20 (Fossil Creek).* The USGS 1:24,000 Strawberry quadrangle (1967) covers the approach and shows the flume road, but not the connecting trail.

Access. *At the western end,* from FR 708 at the trailhead 14 miles west of SR 87 at Strawberry (Fossil Springs Road). Paving ends at 2.4 miles; it is a good dirt road beyond, with spectacular views where it descends the face of the canyon. (Pay close attention; persons with fear of heights may have problems, and there have been accidents here.) The trailhead is just before the Irving Power Plant, on the right. *At the eastern end,* from the end of the Mail Trail [#84 on the Coconino Forest] and Fossil Springs Trail [18]).

General Description. The trail immediately descends to Fossil Creek and crosses it at a ford. On the opposite bank it starts a steep, rocky, 400' climb to meet the Flume Road at 0.4 mile. From there it follows the general alignment of the flume, above and below it, with several elevation changes, to the dam at 4.2 miles. Beyond, trail begins and ascends and descends the canyon wall to 4.6 miles, where it meets the Fossil Springs Trail [18]/Mail Trail [84]. Total ascent is about 900'.

Read Down ↓	*Detailed Trail & Road Description*	Read Up ↑
0.00	From the trailhead parking area at 3,820', descend N , then W to Fossil Creek (use care on rocky descent and crossing creek).	4.61
0.04	Cross Fossil Creek on rocks. Trail sign is 50' beyond. Just beyond, go N, zigzagging steeply up rocky trail.	4.57
0.08	Gate in barbed-wire fence. Head W, then start steep ascent to N.	4.53
0.11	Top of rise. Head SW.	4.50
0.12	**Junction:** switchback sharp R (NE; trail of use ahead). Views open.	4.49
0.35	Switchback to L (W), then to R in 400'.	4.26
0.41	**Junction:** just beyond register, foot trail ends at Flume Road [FR 154]. Take it uphill to R. (Road L closed to public.)	4.20

---

[1]As reported in the *Arizona Republic,* November 18, 1999 (page B1). This is the first instance of a reversal of river development in the state, and will lead to enhanced wildlife habitat. The power plants were built shortly after 1900 to power mines and towns from Phoenix to Flagstaff.

0.52 Cross bridge over flume. 4.09
0.68 Flume is just L of road. 3.65
0.82 Hairpin turn to L, then bridge over flume in 55'. 3.79
0.95 Top of rise. Bear L. 3.66
1.03 Hairpin turn to R. 3.58
1.18 Hairpin turn to R. 3.43
1.46 Top of rise in level area with good viewpoint high above flume. 3.15
1.49 Descend L. Pass S-bend in flume. 3.12
1.70 Start descent to below flume. 2.91
1.78 Bottom of descent. Turn R. Small seep on L. 2.83
1.80 Cross under flume twice. 2.81
1.84 Beside flume, ascend gradually. 2.77
1.85 Top of rise. Level. 2.76
1.96 Ascend above flume. 2.65
2.01 **Junction:** bulldozer road descends to R. Continue ascending. 2.60
2.11 Switchback to R, then road rises to E. 2.50
2.19 Switchback to L. 60' to R is viewpoint. Ascend steadily. 2.42
2.22 Top of rise. Bear L, descend (siphon in flume is ahead). 2.39
2.33 Cross bridge over side-canyon, head SE. 2.28
2.38 Top of rise. 2.23
2.46 View R of siphon. 2.15
2.49 Landmark: pass to R of very large white rock formation. 2.12
2.56 Cross big wash. 2.05
2.65 **Junction:** road on R, another in 75'. 1.96
2.69 To R is maintenance shed and viewpoint. 1.92
2.95 Cross cattle guard at top of rise. 1.66
3.18 Cross under flume. 1.43
3.52 Go under flume. 1.09
3.66 Top of rise with cliffs above on L. 0.95
3.80 Solar-powered transmitter on R. 0.81
3.86 Turn R under flume, then level out, heading into treed valley. 0.75
3.97 Bottom of descent in riparian area. Ascend gradually through attractive area. 0.64
4.08 Barbed-wire enclosure on R. 0.53
4.10 **Junction:** trail of use to R. 0.51
4.11 Go under flume, ascend. 0.50
4.15 Solar-powered transmitter on R. 0.46
4.16 *Road ends* at building & dam feeding water into the flume (to R). *Trail starts.* 0.45
4.17 **Junction:** keep L behind building. Enter Fossil Springs Wilderness. 0.44
4.21 **Junction:** spur on R descends to Fossil Creek and springs. Ascend
       steadily, side-hilling steep valley wall. 0.40
4.27 Top of rise. 0.34
4.34 Above Fossil Springs. The flow is impressive (over a million gallons/hour). 0.27
4.36 **Junction:** trail of use on R, to creek. Wilderness sign in 150' 0.25
4.42 **Junction:** R to creek. 0.19
4.45 **Junction:** trail of use half-L. 0.16
4.49 Camping area on R. Attractive area. 0.12
4.52 Turn L, ascend for 150'. 0.09
4.61 Bottom of descent. **Junction:** Fossil Springs Trail/Mail Trail [18/84] ahead,
       and sharp R to Fossil Springs in 325'. Elevation 4,400'. 0.00

Ahead, the Fossil Springs Trail [18] (also the Mail Trail [84] on the Coconino National Forest) leads to the trailhead at FR 784 off FR 708 in 3.2 miles.

Good Enough Trail WEST to EAST

Manzanita Drive to Pine Canyon Trail [26]

Introduction. The Pine Canyon Trail is a long day's trip to the Rim, and very strenuous to make in both directions if returning to your starting point. To get around private property, it makes a long detour along the flank of Milk Ranch Point. The Good Enough Trail shortens the distance by giving access at an intermediate point.

Maps. *Our Map 2 (Highline 2: Pine).* The USGS 1:24,000 Pine quadrangle (1973) covers the Pine Canyon Trail, but not this trail.

Access. *At the western end,* from Manzanita Drive road end. From SR 87 in Pine, turn east on Whispering Pines (14.75 miles north of the junction in Payson). Drive north 1.5 miles (partly gravel) to Manzanita, then steeply right, uphill, to 1.6 miles where there is an obvious access point at the end of the road. *At the eastern end,* from Pine Trailhead 1.7 miles, from Camp LoMia 2.6 miles. Marking is with occasional arrows. *Note that this is not a Forest Service system trail, and that access or parking in the future may be denied.*

General Description. This trail goes initially through jumbled terrain, starting a steady ascent at 0.25 mile. Wild Bill's Spring is reached just beyond. From there the trail makes a steady ascent through the forest, with few breathers, to its junction with the Pine Canyon Trail at 0.75 mile. Total elevation gain is 500'.

Read Down ↓	Detailed Trail Description	Read Up ↑
0.00	From Manzanita Drive Trailhead (5,700'), head E thru gate in fence. At 170' bear L, then at 340' turn R and descend.	0.76
0.10	Ascend ESE.	0.66
0.12	Top of rise; descend.	0.64
0.14	Bottom of descent. Ascend.	0.62
0.18	Cross small wash. Head E, ascending (5,760').	0.58
0.21	Top of rise (5,780'). Swing S, then E.	0.55
0.23	**Junction:** turn L here and ascend.	0.53
0.24	**Junction:** keep L where trail enters R (from previous side-trail).	0.52
0.26	"Wild Bill's Spring" (5,780'). Switchback to R (S).	0.50
0.27	**Junction:** turn L (steadily uphill) at cairn (no sign), then swing E & ENE.	0.49
0.39	Turn L (N) (5,880').	0.37
0.42	Level briefly, then switchback to R (E).	0.34
0.44	Turn L (ENE).	0.32
0.47	Turn R (SE) (5,910').	0.29
0.49	Bear L (E).	0.27
0.56	Turn R (S) (6,000').	0.20
0.58	Bear L (E), then ENE and NE, ease.	0.18
0.66	Switchback to R (S).	0.10
0.68	Switchback to L; ascend to NE.	0.08
0.74	Ease grade of ascent.	0.02

0.76 **Junction:** Pine Canyon Trail [26] L & R (6,140'). To the R, the Pineview Trail [28] is 1.61 mi, passing Upper Dripping Springs at 0.38 mi and Lower Dripping Springs at 0.52 mi. Pine Trailhead is at 1.68 mi. To the L, Camp LoMia junction is at 2.6 mi. 0.00

Houston Loop COUNTERCLOCKWISE

From Chaparral Pines

Introduction. In 1996 this trail was constructed as part of an increased local interest in equestrian trail opportunities. The Loop is the site of the annual spring Payson Mayor's Cup Bike Race. The name "Houston" comes from pioneers who first used the area for cattle grazing (relatives of Sam Houston, first president of the Texas Republic). (The seismic bunker was part of a network of stations to monitor Chinese nuclear tests.)

Maps. *Our Map 21 (Houston Mesa).* The USGS 1:24,000 Payson North quadrangle (1973) shows the terrain, but not the trail.

Access. 2.4 miles east of Payson town center on SR 87 is a paved road on the left to the Chaparral Pines subdivision. At 1.3 miles on the end of this road there is a paved circle with very limited parking at the trailhead (near house address #808). Please observe private property signs.

General Description. The trail takes a circuitous route at first, to the northwest, then swings around to the east past a seismic bunker to a junction of vehicleways with the Shoofly Trail at 0.3 mile. Turning back briefly towards the subdivision, the trail then turns sharply northeast to the Loop at 0.6 mile. Heading south, it passes another seismic bunker and at 0.9 mile heads east and drops northerly and then easterly into the Houston Creek valley to cross it at 1.7 miles and Mayfield Creek at 2.3 miles. It then winds north with some views to re-cross Houston Creek at 3.5 miles. From here the trail; heads almost straight southwest to the start of the Loop at 4.4 miles. Return to the start is at 5 miles. Total elevation gain is about 120'. Some GPS locations (in UTM format, NAD 1927) are provided.

Cautions. The trail has more up and down sections than the map would indicate; therefore it is important for hikers to allow enough time. The Forest Roads are not posted with numbers; use care to follow signs on carsonite posts or other marking, as unauthorized trails have been created.

Read Down ↓	Detailed Trail Description	Read Up ↑
0.00	From the TH, head NW (4,820').	4.37
0.14	Pass seismic bunker site (mound) on L. Bear R (E).	4.23
0.33	**Important junction:** sharp L is Shoofly Trail to Houston Mesa Trailhead [GPS 0474655/3791730]. Turn half R.	4.04
0.41	**Junction:** ignore road to gate (private property) on R. Go sharp L, uphill. Views. [GPS 0475040/3791870].	3.96
0.59	**Important junction:** go R on Loop; L is Loop returning. Top of rise.	3.78
0.73	Seismic bunker on L (4WD road on L). Keep R. [GPS 0475100/3791690]	3.64
0.79	Top of rise. [GPS 0475080/3791630]	3.58
0.92	**Junction:** turn L, ignoring road on R. [GPS 0474960/3791450]	3.45
1.10	Top of rise. [GPS 0475240/3791410]	3.27
1.30	**Junction:** ignore trail on R. Bottom of descent; ascend L. [GPS 0475590/3791385]	3.07
1.34	Top of rise. Descend to N. [GPS 0475610/3791425]	3.03

1.45 **Junction:** ignore trail on L. [GPS 0475685/3791600].. 2.92
1.49 **Junction:** ignore trail on L; bear R. [GPS 0475715/3791645] 2.88
1.55 Bear R through ponderosa forest. [GPS 0475850/3791630] 2.82
1.61 Cross creek, and again in 150'. 2.76
1.70 *Cross Houston Creek* and ascend steadily. [GPS 0476060/3791580] 2.67
1.75 Top of rise. 2.62
1.83 Go L, ascending. [GPS 0476140/3791570].. 2.54
1.88 **Junction:** ignore trail on R. 2.49
1.92 Top of rise. 2.45
1.97 **Junction:** go L; ignore trail on R. [GPS 0476450/3791555]10415...................... 2.40
2.04 Ascend. 2.33
2.12 Top of rise. [GPS 0476410/3791800] 2.25
2.22 **Junction:** trail on L; keep R. [GPS 0476395/3791945]................................... 2.15
2.32 *Cross Mayfield Creek.* [GPS 0476530/3791960]... 2.05
2.35 Go L. 2.02
2.40 Go E, then N (views). [GPS 0476610/3791950]... 1.97
2.48 **Junction:** avoid trail R; go L. [GPS 0476640/3791985]................................... 1.89
2.63 Descend straight road. 1.74
2.66 Bottom of descent. 1.71
2.68 Top of rise. [GPS 0476670/3792430]... 1.69
2.78 **Junction:** two routes, steeper on R. Go L. [GPS 0476700/3792575]................. 1.59
2.85 Top of rise. 1.52
2.89 Cross small creek. [GPS 0476600/3792715] 1.48
2.92 Cross creek. [GPS 0476585/3792750]... 1.45
2.95 Top of rise. Bear L (W). [GPS 0476575/3792810].. 1.42
2.99 Top of rise. 1.38
3.00 Cross creek. [GPS 0476500/3792845] 1.37
3.04 Bottom of descent. 1.33
3.09 **Junction:** ignore trail on R. Keep straight ahead. [GPS 0476390/3792870]........ 1.28
3.17 Top of rise. 1.20
3.26 Top of rise. 1.11
3.28 **Junction:** avoid trail sharp L. [GPS 0476075/3792915...................................... 1.09
3.32 Bottom of descent. [GPS 0476020/3792910]... 1.05
3.38 Top of rise. [GPS 0476950/3792940] 0.99
3.43 Top of rise. 0.94
3.49 **Junction:** ignore vehicleway on R. [GPS 0475800/3792960]............................ 0.88
3.51 *Cross Houston Creek.* Ascend steeply to W. [GPS 0475740/3792950]............... 0.86
3.56 **Junction:** avoid vehicleway on R. Top of rise. Descend to L. Views. 0.81
3.61 Bend R (SW), ease. [GPS 0475665/3792415].. 0.76
3.73 Cross creek. 0.64
3.74 Top of rise. 0.63
3.80 **Junction:** trail angles to L; keep R on narrower trail.
      [GPS 0475555/3792455][no sign here] 0.57
3.82 Descend steeply; cross small creek; ascend steeply. 0.55
3.83 Descend steeply in straight line. 0.54
3.88 **Junction:** road from L rejoins. 0.49
3.90 **Junction:** ignore road on L. 0.47
4.02 Cross side-creek; major creek is on L. 0.35
4.03 **Junction:** ignore road on R. 0.34
4.05 Cross creek. [GPS 0475665/3792280].. 0.32
4.15 **Junction:** ignore road on L. [GPS 0475150/3792165]................................... 0.22
4.37 **Junction:** Back at starting point (at 0.59 mi). 0.00

Shoofly Trail CLOCKWISE

Horse Camp Trailhead to Houston Loop Trail

Introduction. In 1996 this trail was constructed as part of an increased local interest in equestrian trail opportunities.

Maps. *Our Map 21 (Houston Mesa).* The USGS 1:24,000 Payson North quadrangle (1973) shows the terrain, but not the trail.

Access. *At its western end,* from Houston Mesa Trailhead off Houston Mesa Road. From the junction of SR 87 & 260 in Payson, take SR 87 north for 1.8 miles to paved Houston Mesa Road (FR 199), and turn right. The Houston Mesa Horse Camp and Campground are another 0.3 mile, and the Houston Mesa Trailhead is another 1 mile from SR 87. Enter the Trailhead parking area on the right. *At its southeastern end*, from the Houston Mesa Trail at 0.33 mile.

General Description. This trail is described from the Trailhead rather than from the Campground, although it can be accessed from the latter point by another section of (horse) trail 0.7 mile long. From the Trailhead, this trail leads up and down for 1.3 miles along the flank of Houston Mesa with occasional views. In another 0.9 mile of recent trail construction it reaches an old road and heads southeast for 0.7 mile to end at the Houston Loop Trail, a total of 3.6 miles. Total elevation gain is about 150'. (Because of possible confusion, some UTM GPS locations, NAD 1927, are shown.)

Cautions. The trail has more up and down sections than the map would indicate; therefore it is important for hikers to allow enough time. The Forest Roads are not posted with numbers; use care to follow signs on carsonite posts and cairns, as confusing unauthorized trails have recently been constructed.

Read Down ↓	Detailed Trail Description	Read Up ↑
0.00	Houston Mesa Horse Camp road.	0.71
0.03	Pass thru gate in barbed-wire fence. [GPS 0471485/3791990]	0.68
0.17	**Junction (4-way):** NDT crosses. Ascend.	0.54
0.28	Top of rise.	0.43
0.36	Bottom of descent.	0.35
0.46	**Junction:** ignore trail sharp R. [GPS 0471935/3792015]	0.25
0.71	**Junction:** trail to Houston Mesa Trailhead sharp L (300'). Keep R (5,080').	0.00
0.00	From the Houston Mesa TH, head E (5,080'). [GPS 0471635/3792530]	2.90
0.06	**Junction:** trail R to Horse Camp Campground in 0.7 mi. Keep L. [GPS 0471810/3792305]	2.84
0.08	Descend steadily to L.	2.82
0.10	Cross wash. [GPS 0471820/3792300]	2.80
0.18	Turn L. [GPS 0471940/3792230]	2.72
0.26	Top of rise. [GPS 0472110/3792270]	2.64
0.29	Bottom of descent. [GPS 0472140/3792310]	2.61
0.33	Top of rise. [GPS 0472120/3792290]	2.57

0.42   Cross wash (upper end of Goat Camp Canyon). [GPS 0472280/3792215] 2.48
0.46   **Junction:** keep R on parallel trail. [GPS 0472305/3792200] 2.44
0.51   **Junction:** rejoin main trail. [GPS 0472335/3792230] 2.39
0.52   Top of rise. Swing to L. [GPS 0472330/3792245] 2.38
0.54   Cross very small wash. [GPS 0472325/3792270] 2.36
0.55   Top of rise. [GPS 0472345/3792280] 2.35
0.59   Cross small wash. [GPS 0472310/3792310] 2.31
0.77   Gate in barbed-wire fence. [GPS 0472650/3792355] 2.13
0.84   Descend gradually. [GPS 0472765/3792425] 2.06
0.89   Cross small wash. [GPS 0472835/3792425] 2.01
1.00   **Junction:** turn sharp L onto vehicleway. Pass rocks 125' to R.
       [GPS 0472990/3792465] 1.90
1.05   Cross thru barbed-wire fence. [GPS 0472960/3792510] 1.85
1.09   **Junction:** turn R, head E. [GPS 0472945/3792600] 1.81
1.34   **Important junction:** keep *straight ahead for this trail.*
       [GPS 0473305/3792745] 1.56
1.39   Cross very small wash. 1.51
1.54   Cross large wash (Lockwood Gulch). Go L in it, then R out of it. ....
       [GPS 0473320/3792770] 1.36
1.58   Cross wash. 1.32
1.59   Cross wash. 1.31
1.66   Cross wash. 1.24
1.67   Bear L. 1.23
1.78   Ascend to cross very small wash. 1.12
1.83   **Junction:** NDT on L. 1.07
1.99   Switchback to R. [GPS 0474060/3793015] 0.91
2.11   Go thru gate in fence. [GPS 0474180/3792855] 0.79
2.20   **Junction:** go R here [GPS 0474270/3792750]. 0.70
2.90   **Junction:** Houston Loop Trail, R 0.33 mi to Chaparral Pines TH, straight ahead
       leads to Houston Loop (4,860'). 0.00

[178] Bear Flat-Pleasant Valley Trail
[186] Mescal Ridge Trail

Introduction. The Hellsgate Wilderness Area lies east of Payson, south of SR 260, and west of FR 200. Trail [37] crosses the Wilderness, but is too long and rugged for a day trip for most hikers. This section describes the only easy trip in the Wilderness from Payson. The first part is actually on the Bear Flat-Pleasant Valley Trail [178]. There are very fine views of an unspoiled area on this very feasible day trip. Sections are rocky and steep. In some open areas care must be exercised to find the correct trail route.

Maps. *Our Map 22 (Mescal Ridge).* The USGS 1:24,000 Promontory Butte quadrangle (1973) covers the approach and the trail, but the very beginning is now different.

Access. From Payson, drive 14.1 miles east on SR 260, past the Ponderosa Campground road, and turn right onto the Thompson Draw-Bear Flat Road (FR 405). The paving soon ends past a cattle guard, and a creek (usually dry) is crossed at 0.9 mile. At 1.2 miles is a junction with FR 405A on the right; turn left. The Bear Flat Road is in fairly good condition. After it crosses Bearhide Canyon, it descends 500' down the Tonto Creek canyon wall with excellent views and several hairpin turns to end at the trailhead and camping area at 4.4 miles. Use care on narrow, steep sections, especially when meeting another vehicle. From the trailhead sign, descend to the creek bank. However, the creek can be difficult to cross (the road crosses the creek, but onto private land, and there is no practical way back to public land along the bank). The best crossing, if you do not want to wade, is about 200' downstream. On the other side, you will have to head upstream through the brush to the trail.

General Description. Once on the trail, there is a relentlessly steep ascent of 250' up to a crest, then another steep rise to the junction of the two trails at 0.8 mile. From here, the trail leads up and down over the side of Mescal Ridge with one 200' descent and the same for ascent, to the ridge end at 2.7 miles. The trail then descends 140' to end at Horse Pasture Tank at just short of 3 miles. The best views are at about 2.3 miles, from the northeast around to the southeast, with limited views north and west toward the Mogollon Rim. Total ascent is about 950'.

Read Down ↓	Detailed Trail Description	Read Up ↑
0.00	From the trailhead sign, descend 30' to Tonto Creek, then head downstream to cross, and head upstream on the far bank. Elevation 4,960'.	2.94
0.09	Trail sign. Head L (NE) then parallel barbed-wire fence along property line.	2.85
0.15	Steady ascent begins to S. This steepens considerably.	2.79
0.17	Switchback to R (E). (4,960').	2.77
0.37	Wilderness boundary at top of rise in pass. Descend gradually to SSE.	2.57
0.40	Bottom of descent. Ascend steadily, then steeply.	2.54
0.54	Bear R, viewpoint on L. Trail steepens again	2.40
0.61	Switchback to L.	2.33
0.64	Ease a bit; viewpoint toward Mogollon Rim to L.	2.30

0.69 Top of rise (5,460'). Trail leads through a beautiful area on an easy grade 2.25
0.83 **Junction:** Bear Flat-Pleasant Valley Trail [178] goes L toward Pleasant Valley;
      keep R on Mescal Ridge Trail [186]. Elevation 5,580' 2.11
0.86 Top of rise. Trail narrows... 2.08
0.89 Bottom of descent. 2.05
0.94 Top of rise. 2.00
1.12 Top of another rise. 1.82
1.22 Mescal Ridge Tank on R. Descend rocky trail. 1.72
1.34 CAUTION! Bear R in open, rocky area to find trail. 1.60
1.37 Bottom of descent (5,520'). 1.57
1.50 Top of rise (5,610'). Descend to NW, then swing L (W) down rocky trail
      with views of Mescal Ridge ahead. 1.44
1.64 **Junction:** ignore trail of use on R. Continue steep descent. 1.30
1.81 Bottom of descent. 1.13
1.93 Stock enclosure to left behind barbed-wire fence (5,420'). Swing to L around it. . 1.01
1.98 Start steady ascent up side of next part of ridge. 0.96
2.24 Top of rise. 0.70
2.36 Good views NE and E to Christopher Mtn and toward Pleasant Valley.
      (NOTE: there is little to be gained in going past this point for views.) *0.58*
2.54 Scout Tank on L (5,530'). CAUTION! Head up to S (follow cairns), not to L
      to find trail; there are many confusing stock trails in the area. 0.40
2.70 Top of rise on end of wooded ridge (5,610'). Trail descends 140' from here. 0.24
2.94 Trail ends at Horse Pasture Tank (5.480'). 0.00

[622] Rim Lakes Vista Trail

This trail leads along the Rim itself, connecting various viewpoints along the eastnmost section of the Rim Road [FR 300]. It can often be seen from the road.

Unfortunately, insect infestation and drought have seriously damaged the beautiful ponderosa pine forest and in 2003-2004 substantial salvage logging was under way. The trail is paved in places and in those areas barrier-free, but it has no fence to protect the unwary from the steep drop-off, so caution is advised.

The trail itself is not measured and described here due to its present condition.

Map. *Our Map 17 (Highline 17: 260 Trailhead).* The USGS 1:24,000 Woods Canyon quadrangle (Provisional Edition, 1990) covers the area but does not show the trail.

[43] Barnhardt Trail

Introduction. If you want a real treat, try this trail (at least its lower sections) on a nice day. The lower portion is suitable for hikes with children. Excellent views start at just over 1 mile. Construction was through a very difficult canyon area — imagine the work involved in locating a feasible route! (The name of the canyon and trail comes from an early settler who had a ranch at the canyon's foot.) Although described in other guidebooks due to its well-deserved popularity, this is the first fully detailed published description.

Maps. *Our Map 23 (Barnhardt Canyon).* The USGS 1:24,000 Mazatzal Peak quadrangle (1972) covers the approach and shows the complete trail location accurately.

Access. *At the eastern end,* from FR 419, 12.6 miles south of Payson. This dirt road ascends for 4.8 miles to the parking area and is normally accessible by 2WD vehicles using care. The road itself provides fine views. *At the western end,* from the Matzatzal Divide Trail [23].

General Description. The trail starts at the parking lot, where there is a good view already. It approaches Barnhardt Canyon on an initially rocky trail with good views starting before 0.5 mile. It enters the Mazatzal Wilderness at 0.9 mile. At 1.2 miles truly exceptional views start. At 1.6 miles it switchbacks into a side-valley and up a ridge to 2.5 miles where a cascade is above the trail. It then climbs above some cliffs to 3.1 miles where the outlet of water-falls is crossed. *Here there are perhaps the most spectacular views in the region.* At 3.5 miles the terrain changes as the trail heads into the upper valley after an ascent of 1,600'. This section has excellent walking, mostly at easy grades. At just over 4 miles is the junction of the Sandy Saddle Trail [231]. There is a sometimes tricky creek crossing at 4.75 miles. The way leads up a few minor ridges and finally turns north at just over 6 miles to reach the Mazatzal Divide (Arizona) Trail [23] at 6.2 miles. Total elevation gain is 1,800'

Geology. There is a good description of the interesting geological formations and features of this trail in Ivo Lucchitta's book *Hiking Arizona's Geology* (pages 150-155).

Cautions. The trail is most suitable for hikers, but has been used by horses. There are very steep drop-offs in places; if you are bothered by heights, you may want to stop where the steep area begins. In or after wet weather the creek at 4.75 miles may be difficult to cross.

Read Down ↓	Detailed Trail Description	Read Up ↑
0.00	From Barnhardt TH (4,210'), the trail leaves at a sign, heading uphill.	6.22
0.02	**Junction:** Shake Tree Trail [44] diverges L, to Y Bar Basin. Continue straight, ascending on rocky trail.	6.20
0.08	Hiker's gate thru barbed-wire fence.	6.14
0.25	Cross small draw.	5.97
0.26	Cross rock field.	5.96
0.29	Cross bouldery wash.	5.93

0.45   Open area, views. Side-hill on good trail into side-valley. 5.77
0.56   Gully. Side-hill on beautiful trail. 5.66
0.85   Round small canyon. 5.37
0.86   Wilderness boundary sign. 5.36
0.94   Views of canyon ahead. 5.28
0.96   **Junction:** where Barnhardt Trail continues, a side-trail diverges *sharp R.*
        [GPS 0459885/3772165]. Elevation 4,500' *Detailed description:* narrow trail
        side-hills down, passing a steep slumped area in 120'. At 0.13 mi it turns L,
        becomes more obscure, and descends a rocky area to reach and cross a
        pipeline at 0.15 mi. From here the faint trail descends to 0.18 mi where there
        is a flat area ahead marked by an old dead tree. Cross this tree and descend
        steeply to the creek bottom (use care) at 0.26 mi. Garden Spring (permanent)
        is about 350' to W here, in a rough, bouldery, brushy area just before a canyon
        (elevation 4,220', elevation loss 280'). 5.26
0.98   *Excellent view of canyon.* 5.24
0.99   Cross small creek. 5.23
1.05   Cross rock field. 5.17
1.08   Enter forest. 5.14
1.12   Out of forest on impressively rugged route. Notice folded rock strata above. 5.10
1.15   *Fantastic viewpoint* (use care on steep drop-offs near here). 5.07
1.18   Descend. 5.04
1.21   Bottom of descent. 5.01
1.23   Go up rocks with fine views. 4.99
1.33   Enter forest briefly. 4.89
1.37   Viewpoint (4,630'). 4.85
1.52   Almost level trail. 4.70
1.58   Turn sharp L above side-valley; waterfall below (4,740'). Ascend crest. 4.62
1.62   Go to L of crest. Caution! 4.58
1.68   Switchback to R (4,840'). Open views. 4.52
1.73   Cross crest. 4.47
1.85   Switchback to L. 4.35
1.94   Switchback to R. Excellent viewpoint (4,940'). 4.28
2.06   Shaded, level area. 4.16
2.08   Switchback to L (5,030'). 4.14
2.17   Switchback to R. Viewpoint. Make steady climb over rocks. 4.05
2.25   Switchback to L. 3.97
2.28   Switchback to R (5,150'). Cross rocky slope. 3.94
2.37   Level area, then gradually ascend again, with care. 3.85
2.48   Top of rise (5,270'). 3.74
2.49   Cross small creek. Cascade is above (after wet weather). 3.73
2.50   Start steep ascent. 3.72
2.52   Zigzag steeply up. 3.70
2.62   Switchback to L. Good viewpoint; trail visible below. Go up rocks. 3.60
2.72   Steep ascent up rocks. 3.50
2.79   Top of rise (5,540'). 3.43
2.80   Swing L at viewpoint; rock shelter on L. 3.42
2.83   Bottom of descent. Ascend gradually into side-valley. 3.39
2.87   Top of rise. 3.35
2.88   Cross small creek. 3.34
2.95   Level out on other side of creek. Bear L up rockier trail. 3.27
3.10   Top of rise (5,580'). Falls ahead in slot canyon. 3.12
3.14   Cross outlet of falls. Ascend N on rocky trail. Views are continuous. 3.08
3.22   Cross rock field. 3.00

3.35	Views E. Cross crest, swing L of it.	2.87
3.43	Cross rock field.	2.79
3.50	Top of rise (5,830'). Swing L at end of crest. Views of N end of Mazatzal	
	Mountain. Terrain changes; head into high valley with easy walking.	2.72
4.05	**Junction:** Sandy Saddle Trail on R, descending. Sign says "Divide Trail 3".	2.17
4.15	Cross small creek.	2.07
4.29	Round end of ridge.	1.93
4.38	Descend gradually into valley.	1.84
4.48	Swing L at small creek.	1.74
4.54	Swing L into big valley.	1.68
4.63	NDT descends steeply to R down to area used for camping.	1.59
4.67	Cross small creek.	1.55
4.75	Cross major creek (may be difficult after wet weather or in spring) (5,900').	
	Ascend thru beautiful ponderosa forest.	1.47
5.13	Emerge from forest.	1.09
5.18	Turn L into next valley.	1.04
5.28	Cross small creek.	0.94
5.37	Turn R.	0.85
5.46	Turn R.	0.76
5.47	Cross end of ridge.	0.75
5.49	Cross end of ridge, side-hill down.	0.73
5.60	Cross small creek.	0.62
5.62	Cross small creek.	0.60
5.71	Turn end of minor canyon.	0.51
5.77	End of small ridge.	0.45
5.83	End of small ridge.	0.39
6.07	Turn R (N).	0.15
6.22	**Junction:** Barnhardt Saddle at 6,000'. Mazatzal Divide Trail [23] L & R.	
	Limited views to W here.	0.00

Chilson Camp (camping and water) is about a mile north. The classic and *very strenuous* circuit trip around Mazatzal Peak (7,903') continues south to Windsor Spring Saddle in another 3.25 miles, then east through Y Bar Basin on Shake Tree Trail [44] back to Barnhardt Trailhead, a total of some 16.7 miles.

NEWS FLASH!!! As this went to press, the West's prolonged drought was claiming much of this area. The Willow Fire (started on June 24, 2004 by a lightning strike) burned over 110,000 acres south of the East Verde River in the Mazatzal Wilderness, an area covering much of the Barnhardt Trail, the Divide Trail, and the Shake Tree Trail, and had also burned the Deer Creek, South Fork and Gold Ridge areas. The photos in this book therefore represent a "before fire" status that may not be seen again for many a year.

[46] South Fork Trail EAST to WEST

Introduction. A _rugged_ 6.7 mile trail up the South Fork of Deer Creek into the Mazatzal Wilderness offers isolation and some interesting vegetation, but is not an easy day trip; in fact, except for very fit walkers with a very early start, a vehicle shuttle is recommended. This is _not_ a good horse trail.

Maps. _Our Map 24 (Deer Creek)._ The USGS 1:24,000 Mazatzal Peak quadrangle (1972) covers the trail, but the lower locations are not accurate.

Access. _At the eastern end,_ from Deer Creek Trailhead. From Payson, it is 16.6 miles south on SR 87 to the junction just south of SR 188 (west side) to the trailhead road, and 0.2 mile further to the parking area. _At the western end_, from FR 201 (Mt. Peeley Road), a 4WD road that leaves from old SR 87 (now FR 627) 9.5 miles south of the Deer Creek Trailhead junction and an additional mile on the spur road, at the wide pull-out area at a pass in the ridge. This is a _rough, narrow road._ On it, FR 191 leads right at 3.3 miles, trail [47] right at 6.3 miles, and this trail junction is at 6.7 miles. Allow about 45 minutes to drive up the road.

General Description. The first 2.5 miles are relatively easy walking with many distant views and a moderate ascent. After passing an old ruined cabin at 2.8 miles the trail becomes narrower, and not always easy to find. There are several canyons and few distant views once the steep valley walls close in. The trail is much more rugged than the map or distance indicate. With almost every creek crossing there is a descent and ascent out of the valley, and there are 39 crossings! The creek is usually dry, but occasional pools can probably be found at lower elevations. Total ascent is 2,100', not counting the many brief up and down sections. _[Effect of the Willow Fire of 2004 has been severe. Check with the Forest Service office.]_

Read Down ↓	Detailed Trail Description	Read Up ↑
0.00	Leave Deer Creek TH (3,380'), ascending R [this is actually part of Deer Creek Trail [45]].	6.69
0.30	**Junction:** Trail [47], Gold Ridge Trail, L, 3.3 mi to FR 201. Cross plateau with good views.	6.39
0.45	Gate in barbed-wire fence.	6.24
0.50	**Junction:** Deer Creek Trail [45] on R. Sign for this trail says "FR 201 - 7".	6.19
0.84	Top of rise. Descend rocky area.	5.85
0.99	Top of rise, views.	5.70
1.08	Enter side-creek for 200'.	5.61
1.15	Cross main creek to R.	5.54
1.26	Beside creek; ascend steadily away from creek.	5.43
1.69	Top of rise. Views back to trailhead area and Sierra Anchas.	5.00
1.73	Cross side-creek.	4.96
1.93	**Junction:** trail of use sharp L. Keep straight on thru beautiful semi-open area with large fields of prickly pear cactus. [Probably altered by 2004 fire]	4.76
2.29	Cross creek to L; easy walking.	4.40
2.35	Bare hill above on R, views up valley ahead.	4.34
2.50	Cross creek to R.	4.19
2.55	Cross creek to L.	4.14

2.61	Cross creek to R.	4.08
2.64	Cross creek to L; trail widens.	4.05
2.82	Stone roofless cabin on L (see photo next page). [GPS 0462265/3765590]	3.87
2.85	Rock wall on R.	3.84
2.95	Cross double creek bed.	3.74
3.06	Bottom of descent.	3.63
3.12	Cross open hillside.	3.57
3.21	Cross small side-valley.	3.48
3.33	Cross creek to L, then R in 50'.	3.36
3.37	Cross creek, near large rock.	3.32
3.41	Join creek briefly.	3.28
3.44	Cross creek to L.	3.25
3.47	Wilderness Boundary sign; ascend.	3.22
3.60	Top of rise. Descend steep pitch.	3.09
3.69	Cross side-creek.	3.00
3.71	Cross creek to R.	2.98
3.78	Top of rise.	2.91
3.94	Cross creek to L (brushy).	2.75
3.97	Cross creek to R.	2.72
4.05	Cross creek to L.	2.64
4.14	Steep pitch up.	2.55
4.20	Camping area, bypassing canyon.	2.49
4.25	Top of rise, some views. Descend steep pitch above canyon.	2.44
4.29	Cross creek. Switchback to L in 20'.	2.40
4.44	Cross creek at large boulder.	2.25
4.51	Cross creek to L after side-hilling along it.	2.18
4.53	Landmark: pass flat rock face on L.	2.16
4.55	Top of rise. Descend with drop-off on L. Use care.	2.14
4.56	Cross creek.	2.13
4.59	Cross creek.	2.10
4.65	Cross creek.	2.04
4.69	Top of rise.	2.00
4.72	Cross creek.	1.97
4.74	Switchback to L. Ascend steep pitch.	1.95
4.75	Switchback to L, in 35' to R, then in 25' to L.	1.94
4.82	Top of rise. Some views. Descend steep pitch.	1.87
4.84	Top of rise. Descend steadily into valley.	1.85
4.87	Cross side creek to R. Enter main creek bed.	1.82
4.89	Leave creek on R.	1.80
5.06	Enter rocky creek bed for 75'.	1.63
5.09	Cross creek.	1.60
5.16	Cross creek to R.	1.53
5.20	Cross creek to L, ascend steep pitch.	1.49
5.24	Cross creek to R (many blowdowns).	1.45
5.31	Enter creek on L. Leave creek in 85'.	1.38
5.38	Cross creek.	1.31
5.43	Cross creek.	1.26
5.46	**Junction:** trail of use on R. Parallel creek.	1.23
5.47	Bear R in blowdown area, use care finding trail.	1.22
5.48	Cross creek to L, then again to R in 125'. Follow steep side-valley up to R.	1.21
5.59	Turn sharp L onto side-hilling trail.	1.10
5.66	Cross creek to L.	1.03
5.74	Cross side-valley.	0.95

5.78	Cross side-valley.	0.91
5.88	Cross creek after side-hilling high above creek.	0.81
5.90	Cross creek.	0.79
5.92	Cross creek.	0.77
5.93	Bottom of descent.	0.76
5.99	Cross creek; follow cairns above canyon.	0.70
6.01	Keep R, not up to L. Use care finding trail here near blowdowns.	0.68
6.03	**Junction:** head L around blowdowns, away from old location.	0.66
6.14	Cross creek.	0.55
6.30	Cross valley.	0.39
6.39	Switchback up to L, then immediately to R, then 3 more in 500'.	0.30
6.52	Start ascent to ridge crest.	0.17
6.56	Crest; turn R up it.	0.13
6.61	Pigeon Spring on L; turn R and ascend.	0.08
6.69	FR 201, sign. Elevation 6,080'. To L it is 0.4 mi to Gold Ridge Trail [47], and 6.3 mi to SR 87. To the R, FR 201 leads to Davey Gowan Trail [48] in 0.7 mi, and Deer Creek Trail [45] at Peeley TH at 2.2 mi.	0.00

[47] Gold Ridge Trail EAST to WEST

Introduction. This trail, outside the Mazatzal Wilderness, partly follows the route of an old vehicleway, mostly up a high ridge crest. From 1.5 miles wide views start of the Mazatzal Mountains, the Mogollon Rim to the north, the Sierra Anchas to the east, and the Four Peaks area and Roosevelt Lake to the south. To do the entire trip is not easy unless an early start is made or two 4WD or high-clearance vehicles are used for a shuttle.

Maps. *Our Map 24 (Deer Creek).* The USGS Mazatzal Peak (1972) quadrangle (1:24,000) shows the route; the very beginning is on the Gisela quadrangle, but not in the correct location.

Access. *At the eastern end,* from the Deer Creek Trail [45] 0.3 mile from Deer Creek Trailhead, which is 0.2 mile off SR 87 just south of the junction with SR 188. This point is 12 miles south of Payson. From Deer Creek Trailhead, the trail ascends, switchbacks right, then tops a plateau to reach the start of this trail. *At the western end,* at FR 201, a 4WD road 6.2 miles from the spur off new SR 87 (now FR 627) (about a 35-40 minute drive).

General Description. The first section is easy walking along an old vehicleway for 1.2 miles. Trail then ascends very steadily and sometimes steeply up a series of humps on the ridge to 3.3 miles, where an ascent of a further 750' up a narrow vehiclway (reverting to trail) leads to FR 201 at 6.3 miles. The footway is variable, with some very steep and trenched sections, but it is easy to follow. It is not really suitable for mountain bikes or horses. Views are excellent. Ascent is about 2,000' to the road, 2,750' total elevation gain. *[This area was severely affected by the Willow Fire of 2004.]*

Read Down ↓	Detailed Trail Description	Read Up ↑
0.00	From Deer Creek Trail [45] junction, head W on old wide vehicleway (3,400').	6.29
0.25	Top of rise.	6.04
0.30	Enter flat area (old borrow pit), head across it.	5.99
0.33	Ascend out of pit.	5.96
0.35	**Junction:** ignore another vehicleway that joins, sharp L. *Watch for this on your descent.* Descend gradually to S.	5.94
0.42	Bottom of descent. Ascend gradually, then steadily.	5.87
0.73	Top of rise.	5.56
0.78	Bottom of descent on crest. Ascend hillside.	5.51
0.84	Top of rise.	5.45
0.94	Top of small rise.	5.35
0.96	Bear R (E).	5.33
1.02	Turn L (up) at barbed-wire fence, paralleling it.	5.27
1.15	Gate; go thru it to R.	5.14
1.21	Swing R.	5.08
1.32	Reach crest (trail eroding).	4.97
1.39	Switchback to L. Ascend steeply to L of crest.	4.90
1.48	Trenched section.	4.81
1.51	Top of rise; good views. Continue a rocky ascent.	4.78
1.56	Crest.	4.73

1.59	Switchback to R, then ascend steeply.	4.70
1.61	Turn R (trenched steep sections).	4.68
1.70	Switchback to R (NW).	4.59
1.71	Switchback to L, ease briefly, then ascend steeply.	4.58
1.78	Crest.	4.51
1.97	Top of rise on crest, good views of Mazatzal Peak.	4.32
1.98	Bottom of descent. Rocky stretch.	4.31
2.04	Bear R, ascend steeply.	4.25
2.08	Bear R.	4.21
2.14	Ease ascent, on crest.	4.15
2.28	Top of rise. Descend to sag.	4.01
2.34	Bottom of descent.	3.95
2.39	Head off crest to L.	3.90
2.44	Ascend steeply.	3.85
2.46	Switchback to R, then to L. Steep, rocky trail; use care.	3.83
2.50	Turn L, steep eroded section.	3.79
2.54	Switchback to R.	3.75
2.56	Switchback to L.	3.73
2.61	Top of rise on hump; good views.	3.68
2.68	Bottom of descent.	3.61
2.73	Top of rise. Descend steadily.	3.56
2.79	Bottom of descent. Ascend steadily.	3.50
2.89	Ease grade of ascent.	3.40
2.97	Top of rise.	3.32
3.00	Top of rise. Descend briefly, then go up again.	3.29
3.09	Top of rise. Beyond, easy, almost level trail.	3.20
3.13	Bear L.	3.16
3.24	Top of rise (5,330'). Vehicleway visible ahead. Descend.	3.05
3.27	**Junction:** sharp R is obscure, closed spur road, leading around summit for 0.4 mi, then ending. Ahead, trail becomes a narrow vehicleway, ascending gradually (elev. 5,280') along N side of ridge.	3.02
3.34	Bottom of descent. Ascend steadily.	2.95
3.36	Turn R, ease grade of ascent.	2.93
3.46	Top of rise.	2.83
3.53	Bottom of descent.	2.76
3.94	Top of rise. Excellent views.	2.35
4.18	Landmark: large rocks above on L.. Level area.	2.11
4.37	Cross very small wash, bear R.	1.92
4.91	Bottom of descent.	1.38
5.06	Cross over crest.	1.23
5.16	**Junction:** trail sharp L leads 50' onto crest for views.	1.13
5.20	Top of rise.	1.09
5.27	Top of rise.	1.02
5.45	Sag.	0.84
5.81	**Junction:** reach level area used for camping, with short trail L. Keep R.	0.48
5.95	Camping area on R.	0.34
5.98	Top of rise.	0.31
6.19	Camping area on R.	0.10
6.24	**Junction:** vehicleway splits, both ascend.	0.05
6.29	**Junction:** FR 201 (6,070'). To L it is 6.3 mi to the road spur off of new SR 87; to R, it is 0.4 mi to South Fork Trail [46], 1.1 miles to Davey Gowan Trail [48], and 2.6 mi to Peeley TH (Deer Creek Trail [45])	0.00

[280] Pine Creek Loop

Introduction. Excellent views from the ridge crest towards the front ranges of the Four Peaks and over the southern Mazatzals are offered by this loop which connects with the Ballantine Canyon Trail [283]. Although relatively far from Payson, its views north and (on the average) better weather make it a good half-day or day trip, especially if it's raining or snowing in Payson.

Maps. *Our Map 25 (Pine Creek Loop).* The USGS 1:24,000 Boulder Mountain (1964) quadrangle shows the terrain and the southern leg of the loop, but not the northern, newer one. The Tonto National Forest Map (2001) shows the new segment of this loop.

Access. On the Beeline Highway (SR 87), 21.7 miles north of the junction with Shea Boulevard or 40 miles south of Payson, there was a highway sign misspelled as "Ballentine Trailhead"; this may have been corrected (in 2003 the sign was only present south-bound). The trailhead is 0.1 mile to the right (east).

General Description. The southern (older) segment of this trail gives good views from a ridge-top in only 0.9 mile. It then descends along the crest to a junction with the Ballantine Canyon Trail [283] and the northern segment of this trail at 1.4 miles. Ascent is 750'. The northern segment then side-hills along the Pine Creek valley, and follows it towards the highway which it parallels back to the trailhead at 1.4 miles. In season there is flowing water and a pleasant riparian atmosphere in the creek valley. The total loop is just under 3 miles. The lower section of the Ballantine Canyon Trail [283] offers additional opportunities for views, especially toward the southern Mazatzals, and is included here.

Read Down ↓	Detailed Trail Description	Read Up ↑
	SOUTHERN SEGMENT	
0.00	From TH (2,260'), trail leads thru fence & gate to **junction** of 2 segments.	1.43
0.02	**Junction:** where northern segment heads N, head S on level.	1.44
0.31	Turn to E, then ascend rather flat ridge.	1.15
0.52	Ease grade of ascent, then head thru area of cholla and prickly pear.	0.94
0.90	Top of ridge, excellent views (2,800'). Descend gradually.	0.56
1.11	**Junction:** trail splits, rejoins in 80'.	0.35
1.19	Sag on crest. Ascend.	0.27
1.32	Summit (2,800'). Descend.	0.14
1.43	**Junction:** Ballantine Canyon Trail [283] straight ahead; northern segment of this trail descends on L, back to trailhead in 1.4 mi. Elevation 2,660'.	0.00
	NORTHERN SEGMENT	
0.00	From trailhead, trail leads thru fence and gate (elevation 2,260') and heads N at sign. Parallel highway, ascending gradually.	1.43
0.37	Turn L at minor wash.	1.06
0.45	Top of rise, above Pine Creek. Bear R, descend.	0.98
0.66	Beautiful area. Continue gradual ascent.	0.87
0.85	Small sag. Continue moderate ascent, side-hilling.	0.58

1.43 **Junction:** at sag in ridge (2,660'), Pine Creek Loop continues back to trailhead (see previous segment). On L is Ballantine Canyon Trail [283]. 0.00

From the ridge junction, the **Ballantine Canyon Trail [283]** ascends steadily to a viewpoint in only 0.1 mile, then switchbacks up to a level, excellent camping area at 0.12 mile, then further fine viewpoints are reached at 0.47 mile (3,100'), 0.56 mile, 0.95 mile, and at the start of Ballantine Canyon at 1 mile (3,250'). Beyond, it enters the canyon and leads to Boulder Flat at 3 miles, Rock Tank at 7 miles, and Cline Trailhead at 11 miles. This is an old, rocky, sometimes trenched trail that involves considerable effort for its excellent higher-level views, but the first viewpoint is certainly worth visiting.

Circuit Trips

The following are possible circuits, most of them (except the first two) strenuous. All but one involve the Highline Trail. A car shuttle will make most of these easier if long stretches of road walking are involved.

	Trail/Road	Miles	Maps	Comments
1	Highline Trail [31] from Pine TH; Pine View [28]; Pine Canyon [26]	2.25	2	Easy walking, varied, some views
2	Pine Creek Loop	2.9	25	Excellent views; easy
3	West Webber [228]; Turkey Springs [217], FR 218	6.2	3, 4	
4	Col Devin [290]; [31]; Myrtle [30]; FR 300	10.2	7-10	Very long
5	Babe Haught [143]; [31]; Myrtle [30]; FR 300	9.75	10-12	Very long
6	Babe Haught [143]; [31]; Horton Springs [292]; FR 300	6.5	12-14	
7	See Canyon [184]; [31]; Horton Springs [292]; FR 300	8.0	14, 15	
8	See Canyon [184]; [31]; Drew [291]; FR 300	10.9	15, 16	Very long road walk

Appendix A. Glossary

Cairn. A pile of stones used to mark a trail or trail junction.

Draw. A small valley that narrows as it rises.

Escarpment. A steep slope or long cliff resulting from erosion or faulting, and separating two relatively level areas of differing elevations.

Gorge. A deep narrow passage, often with precipitous rocky sides, enclosed between mountains.

Jog. To "jog" left or right on a trail or road means to join it briefly and then diverge from it.

Non-designated trail [NDT]. A trail of use or previously designated trail that is no longer on the trail system, is not officially maintained, and may be subject to obliteration.

Sag. A minor depression, less dramatic than a pass or canyon.

Side-hill. As a verb, means to angle along a hillside without going straight up. In the East this is sometimes referred to as "slabbing" a hillside.

Switchback. A sudden reversal of direction, like a "hairpin bend" on a road.

Spur. The lateral ridge porojecting from a mountain or mountain range.

Tank. A depression (natural or artificial) that holds water for stock.

Trailhead. Where the trail starts, usually at a road, sometimes at another trail.

Trail of use. A minor or obscure trail developed by irregular usage, not constructed or designated. It often peters out or serves as a short-cut.

Traverse. A long segment of switchbacking trail that leads across a hillside.

Vehicle travelway or *vehicleway.* A term used by some agencies for a way created by unplanned vehicular use.

Wash. An eroded channel that is ordinarily dry except after prolonged or intense rain.

Appendix B.   Resources

Forest Service, USDA, Tonto National Forest

National Forest Office
2324 East McDowell Road, Phoenix 85006
(Phone: 602-225-5200)

Payson Ranger District
1009 E. Highway 260, Payson, AZ 85541
(Phone: 928-474-7900)

Mesa Ranger District [Pine Creek Loop]
5140 E. Ingram Street, Mesa, AZ 85205
(Phone: 480-610-3300)

Tonto Basin Ranger District [Mazatzals]
Highway 88, HC 02, Box 4800, Roosevelt, AZ 85545
(Phone: 928-467-3200)

Forest Service, USDA, Coconino National Forest[1]

National Forest Office
2323 E. Greenlaw Lane, Flagstaff, AZ 86004
(Phone: 928-527-3600)

[1]Blue Ridge/Long Valley Ranger District
HC 31, Box 300, Happy Jack, AZ 86024
(Phone: 928-477-2255)

Red Rock Ranger District
Box 300, 250 Brewer Road, Sedona, AZ 86339
(Phone: 928-282-4119)

Forest Service, USDA, Apache-Sitgreaves National Forest[2]

National Forest Office
309 South Mountain Avenue, US Hwy 180, P.O. Box 640
Springerville, AZ 85938
(Phone: 928-333-4301)

[2]Black Mesa Ranger District
P.O. Box 968, Overgaard, AZ 85933
(Phone: 928-535-4481)

---

[1]Upper section, on Rim west of Tonto Fish Hatchery, including: top of Babe Haught, Myrtle, Col. Devin, West Webber, Turkey Springs, Donahue, Pine Canyon, part of Fossil Springs Trails.
[2]Upper section, on Rim east of Tonto Fish Hatchery, including See Canyon, Drew, Military Sinkhole Trails.

Appendix C. Bibliography

Some of the local history books are hard to obtain. The library in Payson is a good resource.

Adams, B & Neal, E. 1997. *The Kohl's Ranch Story.* (locally published in limited edition.)

Alden P & Friederici, P, et al. 1999. *National Audubon Society Field Guide to the Southwestern States.* New York: Alfred A. Knopf.

Arizona Atlas & Gazetteer, 6th edition. 2004. Yarmouth, ME: DeLorme.

Barnes WC & Granger B. 1988. *Arizona Place Names.* Tucson: University of Arizona Press.

Barstad J. Undated. *The Verde River Sheep Bridge and the Sheep Industry in Arizona.* Phoenix: GA Doyle & Associates.

Bell K. 1985. *The Legend of Kohl's Ranch.* Payson: Central Arizona Publishing.

Bourke JG. 1891. *On the Border with Crook.* New York: Scribners (reprinted 1980).

Bowers JE. 1993. *Shrubs and Trees of the Southwestern Deserts.* Tucson: Southwest Parks and Monuments Association.

Branstetter M. 1976. *Pioneer Hunters of the Rim.* Mesa: Norm's Publishing House.

Chronic H. 1986. *Roadside Geology of Arizona.* Missoula, Montana: Mountain Press Publishing Company.

Dedera D. 1992. *Arizona's Mogollon Rim.* Phoenix: Arizona Highways.

Desert Botanical Garden. 1988. *Desert Wildflowers.* Phoenix: Arizona Highways Magazine.

Dodge NN. 1985. *Flowers of the Southwestern Deserts.* Tucson: Southwest Parks and Monuments Association.

Dollar T & Sieve J. 1998. *Arizona's Wilderness Areas.* Englewood, CO: Westcliffe Publishers.

Farrand J, Jr. & Udvardy MDF. 1994. *National Audubon Society Field Guide to North American Birds: Western Region, 2nd ed.* New York: Alfred A. Knopf.

Kamilli RJ, & Richard SM (eds.). 1998. *Geologic Highway Map of Arizona.* Tucson, AZ: AZ Geological Society & AZ Geological Survey.

Kant CC. 1984. *Zane Grey's Arizona.* Flagstaff: Northland Press.

Karr J. 1949. *Zane Grey: Man of the West.* New York: Grosset & Dunlap.

Krause S. 1994. *Streamside Trails: Day Hiking Central Arizona's Lakes, Rivers, & Creeks.* Tempe, AZ: Pinyon Publishing Co.

Latham L. 1998. *Best Hikes with Children in Arizona.* Seattle: The Mountaineers.

LeCount A (ed.). 1976. *The History of Tonto: A Bicentennial Project.* Punkin Center Homemakers.

Little, EL. 1980. *National Audubon Society Field Guide to North American Trees: Western Region.* New York: Alfred A. Knopf.

Lucchitta I. 2001. *Hiking Arizona's Geology.* Seattle: The Mountaineers.

Mason R. 1997. *Verde Valley Lore.* Scottsdale: L. J. Schuster Co.

Massey P & Wilson J. 2002. *Backcountry Adventures Arizona.* Swagman Publishing: Castle Rock, CO.

Maxa C. 2001: *Arizona's Best Autumn Color: 50 Great Hikes.* Englewood, CO: Westcliffe Publishers.

Maxa C. 2002: *Arizona's Best Wildflower Hikes: The High Country.* Englewood, CO: Westcliffe Publishers.

McMahon JA. 1985. *Deserts (Audubon Society Nature Guides).* New York: Alfred A. Knopf.

Murphy I. 1991. *A Brief History of Payson, Arizona.* Payson: Leaves-of-Autumn Books.

Nations D & Stump E. 1997. *Geology of Arizona, 2nd Edition.* Dubuque, IA: Kendall/Hunt Publishing Company.

Powell C. 1990. *Arizona.* Albuquerque, NM: Univ of New Mexico Press.

Redman CL. 1993. *People of the Tonto Rim: Archeological Discovery in Prehistoric Arizona.* Washington, DC: Smithsonian Institute Press.

Robinson CM. 2001. *General Crook and the Western Frontier.* Norman: University of Oklahoma Press.

Schmitt MF (ed.). 1960. *General George Crook: His Autobiography (2nd Edition).* Norman, OK: University of Oklahoma Press.

Southwest Natural & Cultural Heritage Association. 1990. *Visitors Guide, Coconino National Forest.* Albuquerque, NM: SNCHA.

Southwest Natural & Cultural Heritage Association. 1991. *Visitors Guide, Mogollon Rim: Apache-Sitgreaves, Coconino, & Tonto National Forests.* Albuquerque, NM: SNCHA.

Spellenberg R. 1979. *National Audubon Society Field Guide to North American Wildflowers: Western Region.* New York: Alfred A. Knopf.

Stevenson JL. 1995. *Rim Country Mountain Biking.* Boulder, CO: Pruett Publishing Co.

Stoops ED & Wright A. 1993. *Snakes and Other Reptiles of the Southwest.* Phoenix: Golden West Publishers.

Thrapp DL. 1964. *Al Sieber: Chief of Scouts.* Norman, OK: University of Oklahoma Press.

Tighe K & Moran S. 1998. *On the Arizona Trail: A Guiide for Hikers, Cyclists, & Equestrians.* Boulder, CO: Pruett Publishiong Co.

Trimble M. 1986. *Roadside History of Arizona.* Missoula: Mountain Press Publishing Company.

Varney P. 1980. *Arizona's Best Ghost Towns: A Practical Guide.* Flagstaff: Northland Press.

Walker HP & Bufkin D. 1979. *Historical Atlas of Arizona.* Norman, OK: University of Oklahoma Press.

Way TE. 1960. *Frontier Arizona.* New York: Carlton Press.

Weir B. 2002. *Arizona: Moon Handbooks, 8th Edition.* Emeryville, CA: Avalon Travel Publishing.

Worcester DE. 1979. *The Apaches: Eagles of the Southwest.* Norman, OK: Univ of Oklahoma Press [especially pp. 144-174 "Crook and the Conquest of the Tontos"].

Trip/Correction Reports

Please help us make this a better book in its next printing or edition by informing us of any errors or changes that you find, using these forms

---

I have found the following error or change in the area covered by *Day Hikes & Trail Rides in Rim Country & Payson*:

Area name:_____ Pages: _____ Map No. _____

Details: _____
_____
_____
_____
_____
_____
_____
_____

Send these comments to:

Roger D. Freeman, Box 2033, Point Roberts, WA 98281
e-mail: *rfreeman@cw.bc.ca*
Phone: (604) 263-3900

I have found the following error or change in the area covered by *Day Hikes & Trail Rides in Rim Country & Payson*:

Area name:_____ Pages: _____ Map No. _____

Details: _____
_____
_____
_____
_____
_____
_____
_____

Send these comments to:

Roger D. Freeman, Box 2033, Point Roberts, WA 98281
e-mail: *rfreeman@cw.bc.ca*
Phone: (604) 263-3900

How This Book Was Prepared

For those interested in details, here's how we did it:

Field Data Collection. USGS topographic maps, US Forest Service Geometronics revisions of those maps (intended for internal purposes), and some special maps were used. After the first few years, we purchased and used a Magellan Trailblazer® and then a Garmin® 45XL handheld Global Positioning System to locate waypoints, and plotted these on the base maps. In the past few years the US government has removed the random errors introduced into the GPS system so that locations have become more accurate.

A Thommen® Swiss altimeter, a compass, and a Rolatape® measuring wheel rounded out our technical apparatus.

All trails were measured directly. Accuracy was determined by measuring some trails twice, or in both directions.

Plotting the Trails. In addition to what we could see and measure (length and altitude), locations were plotted using National Geographic's Topo!® CD-ROMs[1] of Arizona, which enabled us to print out a superimposed UTM 100 meter grid.

Review. Countless meetings were held with Forest Service personnel to go over maps and matters of policy. We are very indebted to them for their dedication. Other guidebooks that cover some of the trails were also consulted.

Other Sections. The library in Payson was helpful in our historical research.

Photographs. All photographs in this book were taken by Roger Freeman, initially with a conventional Minolta camera, then with digital Pentax Optio 3-megapixel and Sony 5-megapixel cameras.

---

[1] Copyright 2000, Wildflower Productions, Inc.

Map Legend

NOTE: In urban areas all local streets are not shown

	Described	Not described
Paved road	——	—— cul-de-sac parking area
Unpaved road (driveable by most vehicles)	– – – –	– – – –
Unpaved road (4WD or high-clearance only)	====	====
Main or major trail (with designation)	– – – – [32]	– – – – [32]
Minor or secondary trail		– – – – – –

Approximate boundaries	– – – –
Wash; creek or river	～… ～ ～
Stock tank; spring; lake	• ⌐○ Parsnip Spring ⬭
Building (where shown)	▬
Gate (whether closed or open)	——╪——
Spot elevation	• 7155
Summit of importance	△ 7155
Contour lines	—7155—
Power line	═·═ ⁄·⁄
Campground; Trailhead	CG TH

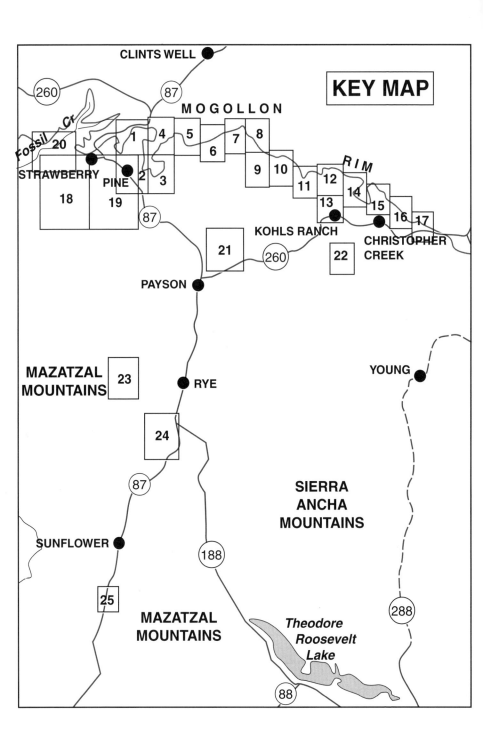

Map 1

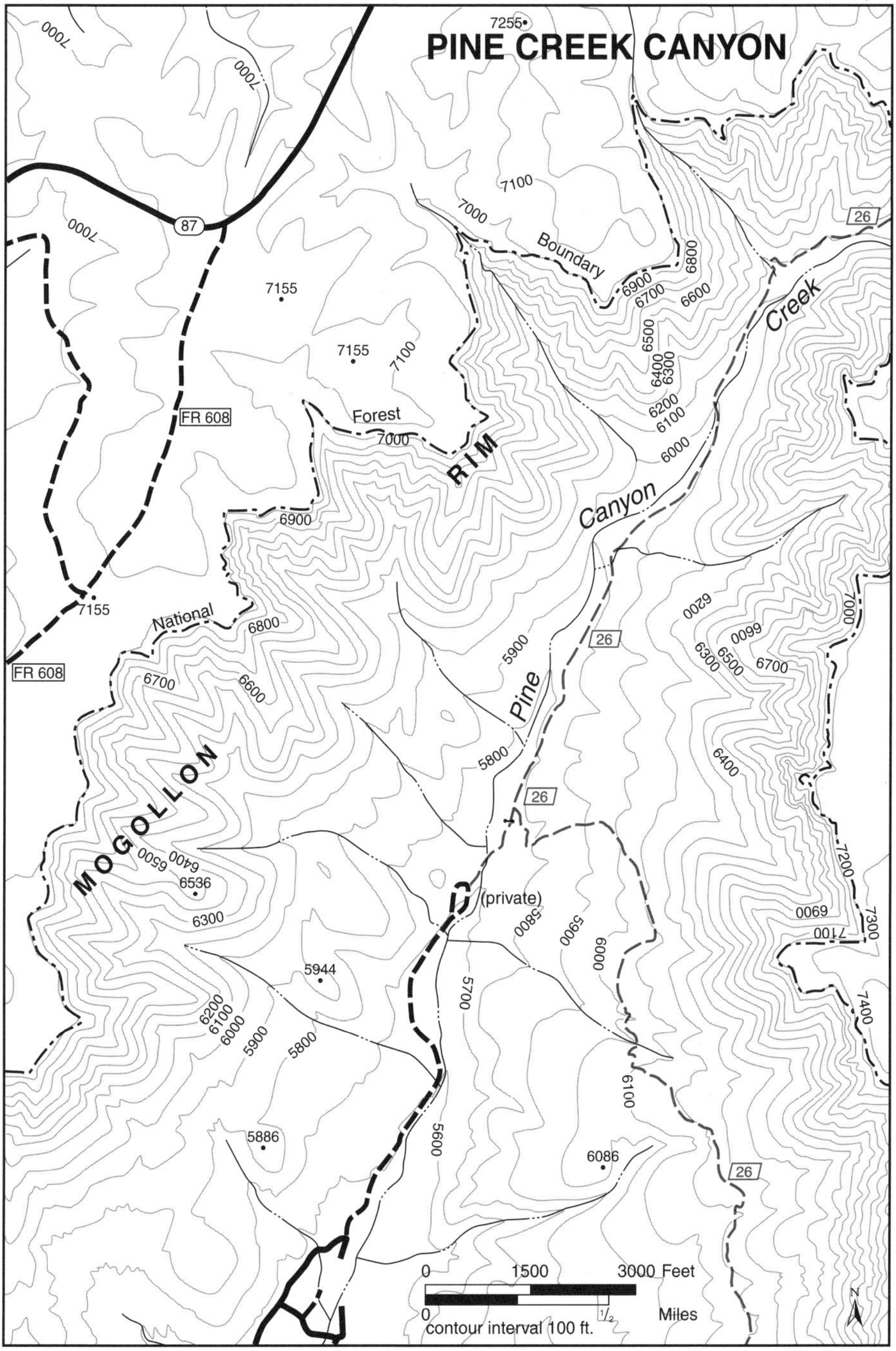

PINE CREEK CANYON

7255

7000

87

7100

7000

Boundary

26

7155

Creek

7155

7100

6900
6800
6700
6600
6500
6400
6300
6200
6100
6000

FR 608

Forest

7000

RIM

Canyon

6900

7155

National

6800

6200
6900
6600
6700

Pine

5900

26

6300
6500
6700

FR 608

6700

6600

6400

MOGOLLON

5800

26

6500
6400

6536

7200

5900

6300

(private)

5800

6000

7100
7300

5944

5700

5900

6000

7400

6200
6100
6000
5900
5800

5600

5886

6100

6086

26

0   1500   3000 Feet

0   1/2   Miles

contour interval 100 ft.

N

Map 2

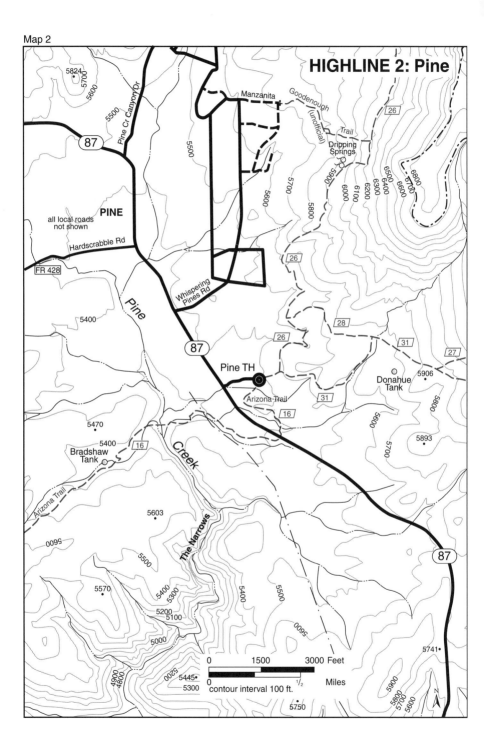

HIGHLINE 2: Pine

Manzanita

Goodenough (unofficial)

Trail

Dripping Springs

26

5824
5700
5600
5500

Pine Cr Canyon Dr

87

5500

5600

5700

5800

5900
6000
6100
6200
6300
6400
6500
6600
6700
6800

PINE

all local roads
not shown

Hardscrabble Rd

FR 428

26

Whispering Pines Rd

Pine

5400

87

26

28

31

27

Pine TH

Arizona Trail

31

16

26

Donahue Tank

5906

5800

5470

5400

16

Bradshaw Tank

Arizona Trail

Pine Creek

5603

The Narrows

5700

5893

5600

5500

5570

5400
5300

5400

5500

5600

5200
5100

5000

4900
4800

5200

5445
5300

5741

0   1500   3000 Feet

0   1/2   Miles

contour interval 100 ft.

5750

5900
5800
5700
5600

N

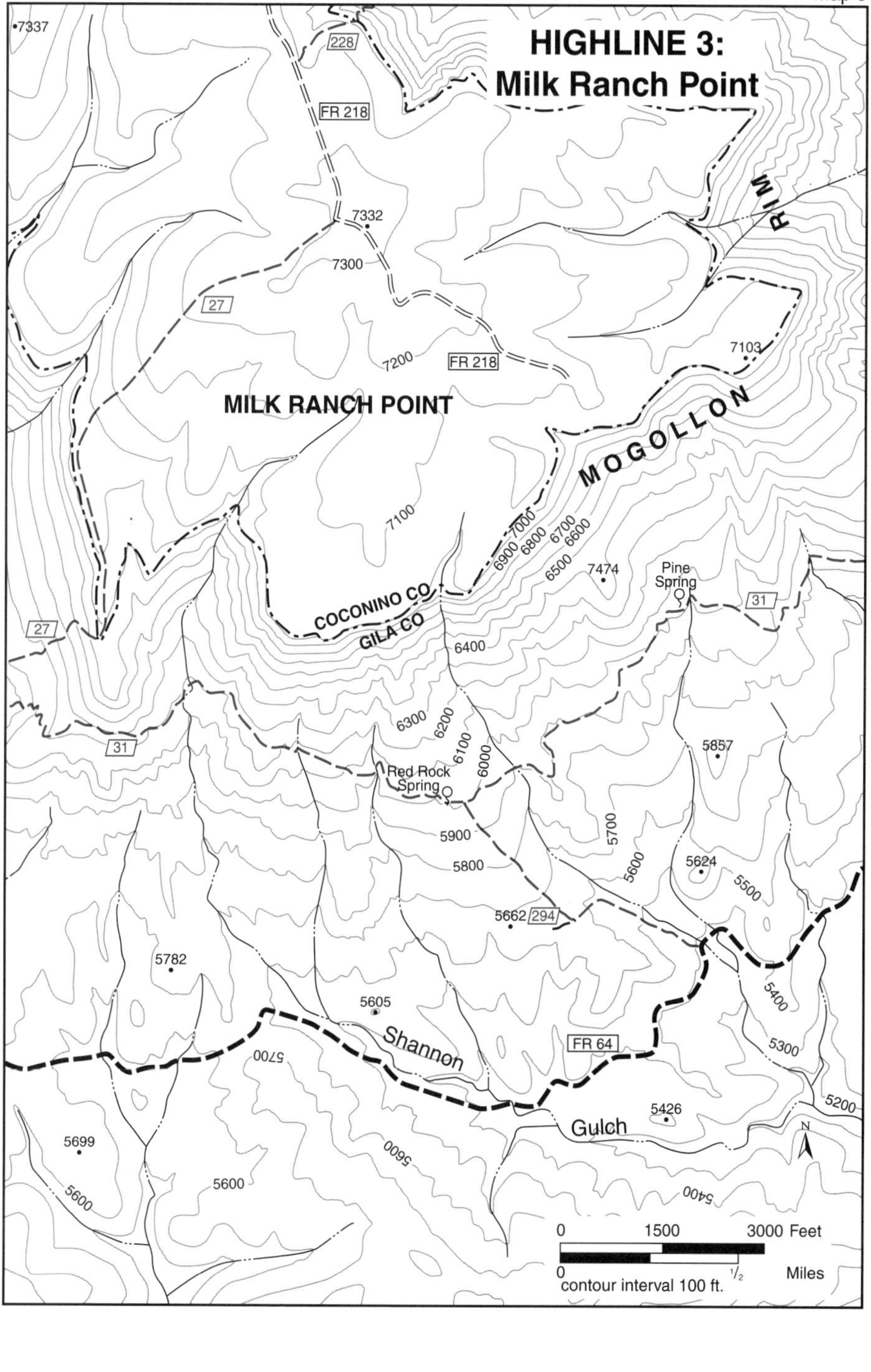

Map 3

HIGHLINE 3:
Milk Ranch Point

•7337

228

FR 218

7332
7300

27

7200   FR 218

7103

MILK RANCH POINT

MOGOLLON

RIM

7100

6900 7000
6800 6700
6500 6600

7474

Pine
Spring

31

COCONINO CO
GILA CO

6400

27

6300 6200
6100
6000

31

Red Rock
Spring

5857

5900

5800

5700

5600

5624

5500

5662 294

5782

5400

5605

Shannon

FR 64

5300

5700

5699

Gulch

5426

5200

N

5600

5600

5400
5400

5600

0   1500   3000 Feet

0   ¹/₂

Miles

contour interval 100 ft.

Map 4

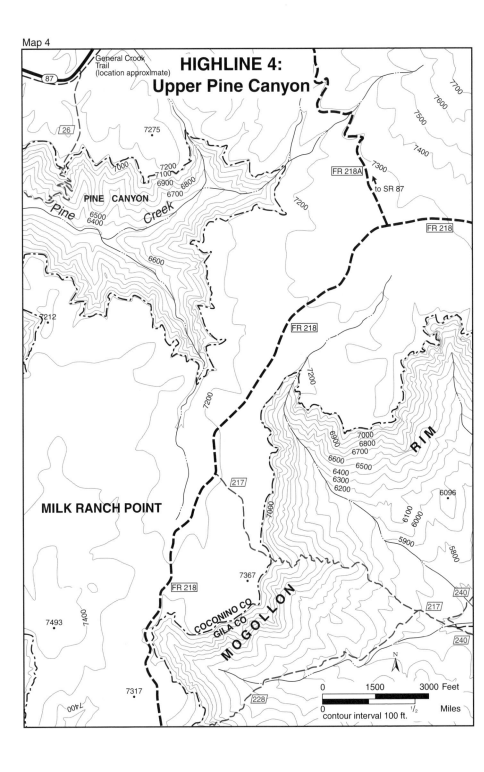

HIGHLINE 4:
Upper Pine Canyon

General Crook Trail
(location approximate)

87

26

7275

PINE CANYON

7000
7200
7100
6900
6800
6700
6500
6400

Pine Creek

6600

7200

FR 218A

7300

7500

7600

7700

7400

to SR 87

FR 218

FR 218

3212

7200

FR 218

7200

7200

RIM

6900
7000
6800
6700
6600
6500
6400
6300
6200

6096

6100
6000

5900

5800

217

MILK RANCH POINT

7000

FR 218

7367

COCONINO CO.
GILA CO.

MOGOLLON

240

217

240

7493

7400

N

0   1500   3000 Feet

7317

228

0   ½

Miles

contour interval 100 ft.

7400

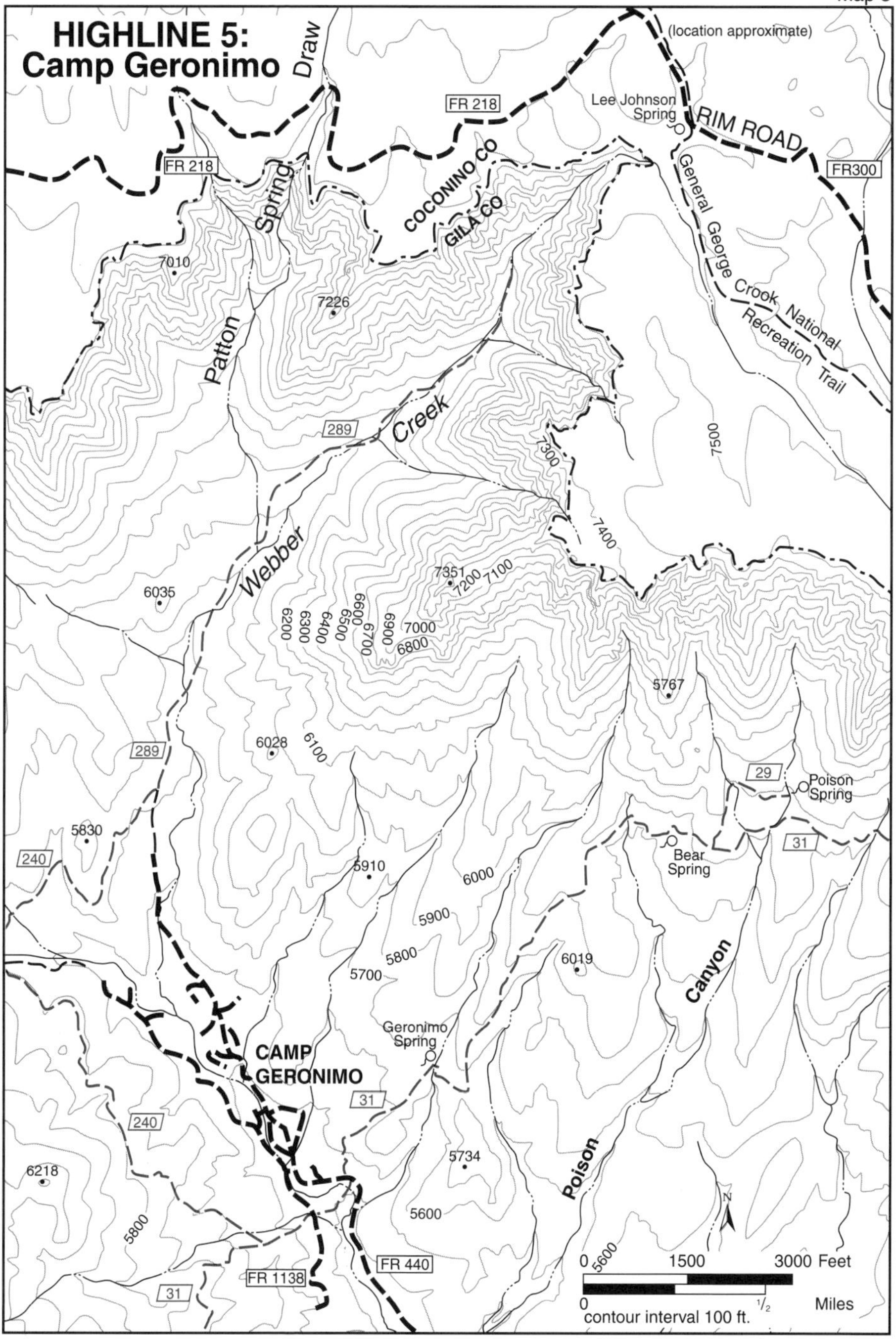

Map 5

HIGHLINE 5:
Camp Geronimo

Spring Draw

(location approximate)

FR 218

Lee Johnson
Spring

RIM ROAD

FR 218

COCONINO CO

GILA CO

FR300

Patton

General George Crook National

Creek

289

7010

7226

Recreation Trail

7300

7500

7400

Webber

6035

7351 7200 7100

6200 6300 6400 6500 6700 6600 6900 7000 6800

5767

6028

6100

289

29

Poison
Spring

5830

31

240

5910

6000

Bear
Spring

Canyon

5900

5800

6019

5700

Geronimo
Spring

CAMP
GERONIMO

31

240

Poison

6218

5734

31

5600

N

0 5600   1500   3000 Feet

5800

FR 440

1/2

31

FR 1138

Miles

contour interval 100 ft.

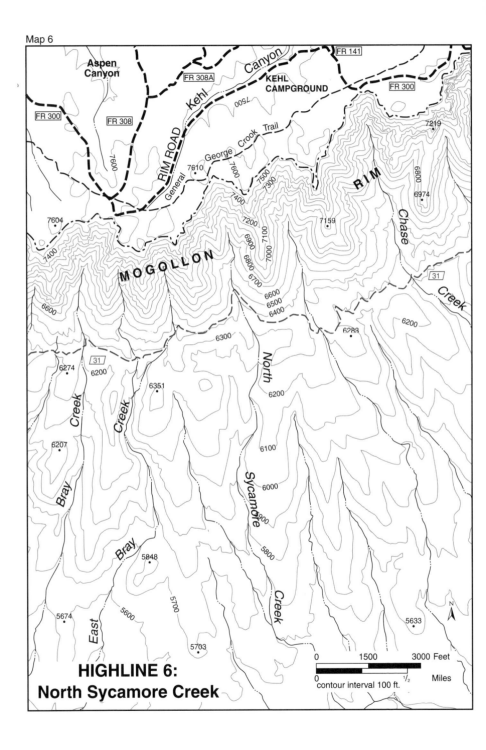

Map 6

Aspen
Canyon

FR 308A

Kehl Canyon

FR 141

KEHL
CAMPGROUND

FR 300

FR 300

FR 308

RIM ROAD

Kehl

7500

George Crook Trail

General

7610

7600

7500

7300

7400

7200

7100

7000

6900

6800

6700

6600

6500

6400

7604

7400

MOGOLLON

6600

6300

6200

6274

31

6200

6351

6207

Bray Creek

Creek

North

Sycamore

6200

6100

6000

5900

5800

Creek

5848

5700

5600

5674

East

Bray

5703

7219

6800

6974

RIM

Chase

31

Creek

6200

6283

7159

5633

N

HIGHLINE 6:
North Sycamore Creek

0   1500   3000 Feet

0   ½   Miles
contour interval 100 ft.

Map 7

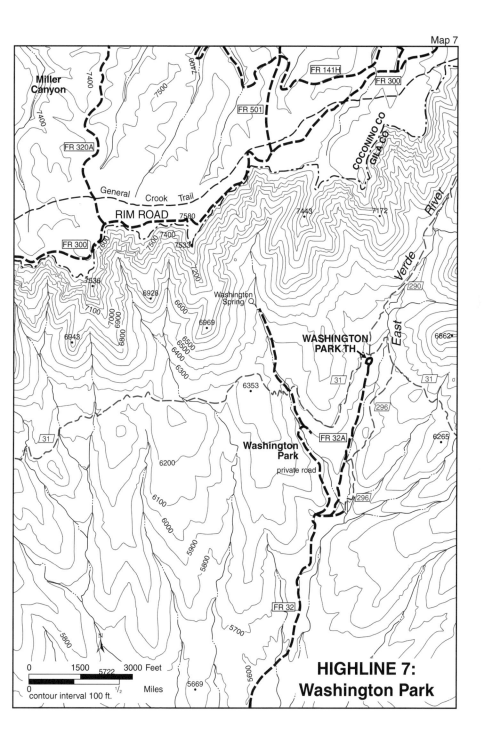

Miller Canyon

FR 141H

FR 300

FR 501

FR 320A

COCONINO CO
GILA CO

General   Crook   Trail

RIM ROAD

7580

7443

7172

FR 300

7533

7536

7200

Washington Spring

290

6928

6600

6969

WASHINGTON PARK TH

East   Verde   River

6943

7100

7000
6900
6800

6500
6400
6300

6862

6353

31

31

296

Washington Park

FR 32A

6265

6200

private road

296

6100

6000

5900

5800

FR 32

5800

N

5700

5600

5669

0   1500   3000 Feet

5722

0   ½   Miles

contour interval 100 ft.

HIGHLINE 7:
Washington Park

Map 8

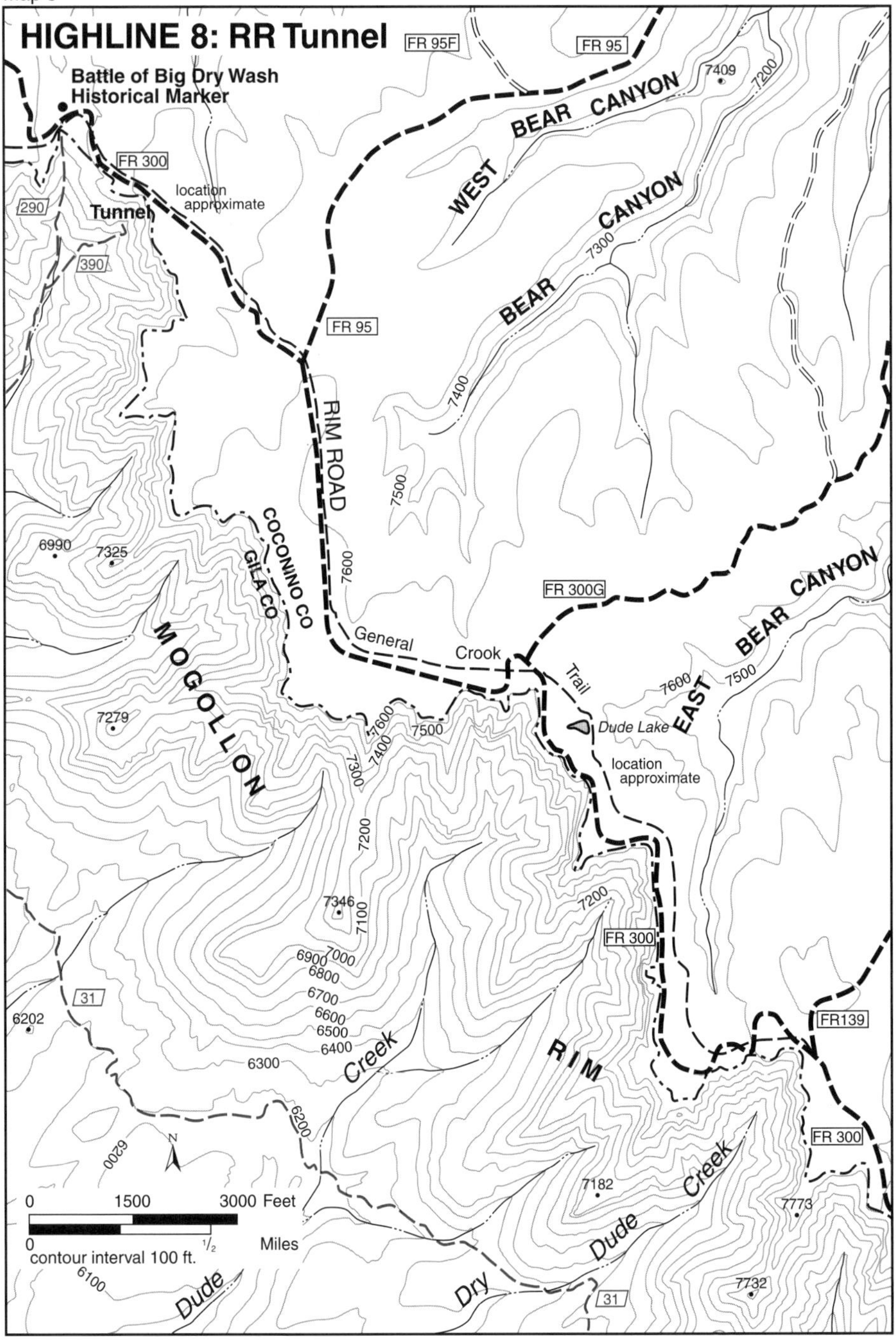

HIGHLINE 8: RR Tunnel

Battle of Big Dry Wash
Historical Marker

FR 95F

FR 95

WEST BEAR CANYON

BEAR CANYON

7409

7200

FR 300

location
approximate

290

Tunnel

390

FR 95

RIM ROAD

7300

7400

7500

7600

COCONINO CO
GILA CO

6990

7325

FR 300G

EAST BEAR CANYON

7600

7500

General   Crook

Trail

MOGOLLON

7279

Dude Lake

location
approximate

7600

7500

7300

7400

7200

7346

7100

7000

6900
6800

7200

FR 300

6700
6600
6500
6400

RIM

FR139

31

6202

6300

Creek

6200

FR 300

N

6200

0   1500   3000 Feet

6100

Dude   Creek

7182

Dry   Creek

7773

0   ½   Miles

contour interval 100 ft.

Dude

Dry

31

7732

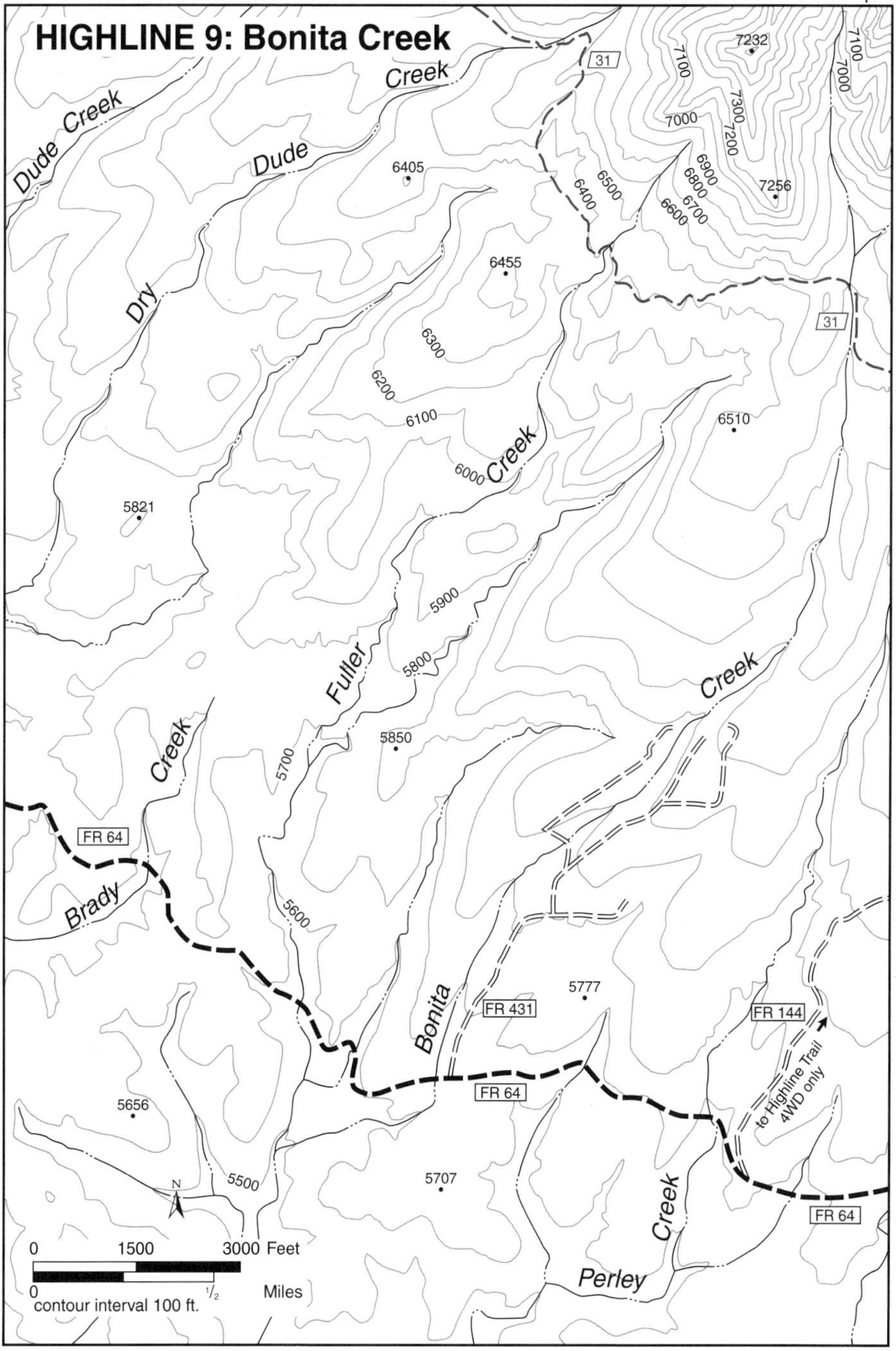

Map 9

HIGHLINE 9: Bonita Creek

Dude Creek

Creek

Dude

Dry

31

7232

7100

7100

7000

7000

7300

7200

7000

6900

6800

6700

6600

6500

6400

7256

6405

6455

31

6300

6200

6100

6000

Creek

6510

5821

5900

5800

Fuller

5850

Creek

5700

Creek

Creek

FR 64

5600

Brady

Bonita

FR 431

5777

FR 144

to Highline Trail
4WD only

FR 64

5656

5500

5707

FR 64

N

0   1500   3000 Feet

0   ½   Miles

contour interval 100 ft.

Perley

Creek

Map 10

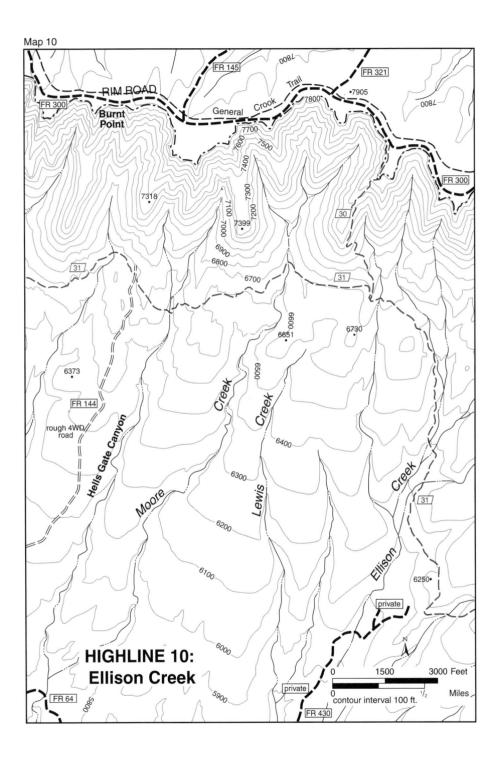

FR 145

7800

FR 321

RIM ROAD

General   Crook   Trail   7800   •7905

FR 300

Burnt
Point

7800

7700

FR 300

7600
7500
7400

7318

7300

30

7100   7200

7000   7399

6900

6800

31   6700

31

•6730

6651

6600

6373

6500

FR 144

rough 4WD
road

Hells Gate Canyon   Creek   Creek

6400

6300   Lewis   Creek

Moore

6200   31

6100   Ellison   Creek

6250•

private

**HIGHLINE 10:
Ellison Creek**

N

0   1500   3000 Feet

6000

private

0   1/2   Miles

5900   contour interval 100 ft.

FR 64   5800

FR 430

Map 11

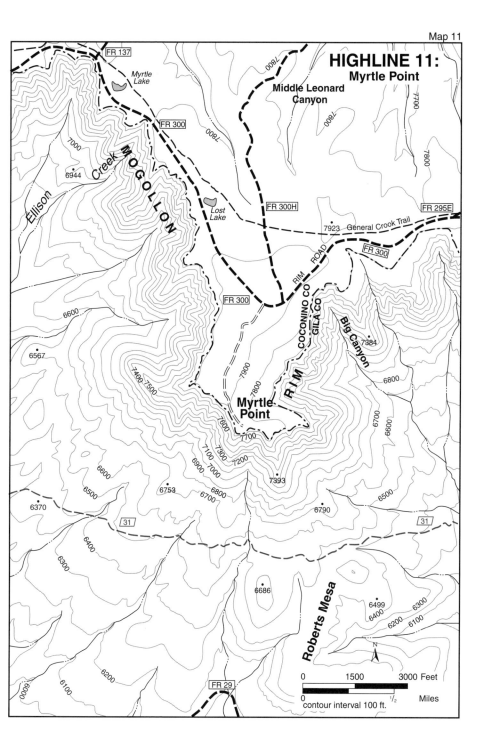

HIGHLINE 11:
Myrtle Point

FR 137

Myrtle Lake

FR 300

Middle Leonard Canyon

7800

7700

7800

Ellison Creek

MOGOLLON

7000

6944

Lost Lake

FR 300H

FR 295E

7923 General Crook Trail

FR 300

7800

RIM ROAD

6600

COCONINO CO

GILA CO

Big Canyon

7384

7900

6567

RIM

7800

6800

7400 7500

Myrtle Point

6700

6600

7800

7700

7100 7300 7200

6900 7000

6600

7393

6500

6500

6753

6800 6700

6370

6790

31

31

6400

6300

6686

6499

6400

6300

6200

Roberts Mesa

6100

N

6200

0   1500   3000 Feet

6100

0   ¹/₂

Miles

6000

FR 29

contour interval 100 ft.

Map 12

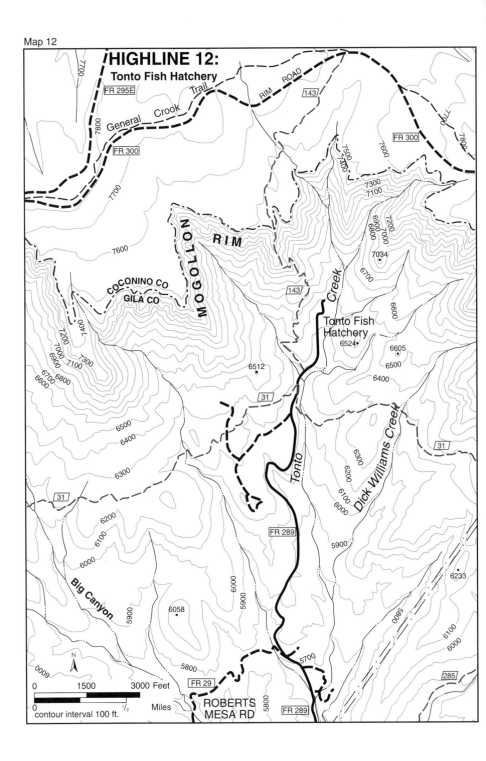

HIGHLINE 12:
Tonto Fish Hatchery

FR 295E

General Crook Trail

RIM ROAD

143

FR 300

FR 300

7700

7800

7700

7600

7500
7400

7600

7300
7100

7200
6900
6800

7000

7034

6700

6600

MOGOLLON RIM

COCONINO CO
GILA CO

143

Creek

Tonto Fish
Hatchery

6524

6605

6500

6400

7400

7200
7000
6900
7100
7300
6900
6800
6700
6600

6512

31

6500
6400

6300

6300

6200
6100
6000

Dick Williams Creek

31

Tonto

31

6200

6100
6000

5900

6233

FR 289

5900

Big Canyon

5900

6200
6100

6000

6000
5900

6058

6000

6100

6000

N

0009

5800

FR 29

5700

5800

285

0   1500   3000 Feet

0   ½   Miles

contour interval 100 ft.

ROBERTS
MESA RD

FR 289

Map 13

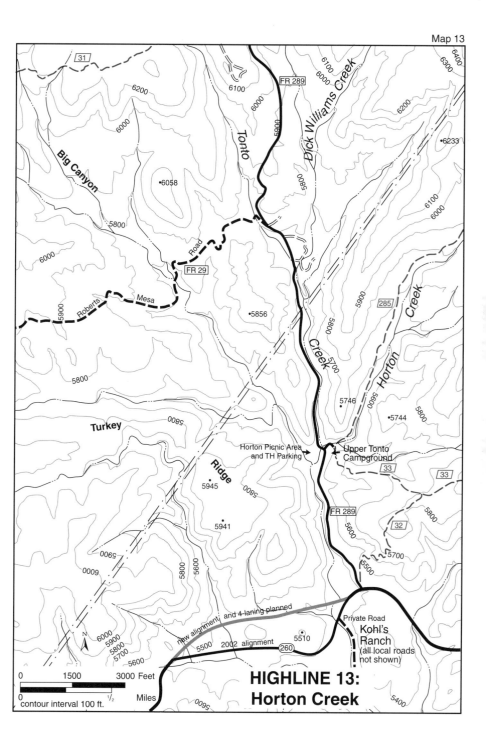

31

FR 289

6400
6300
6100
6000
6200

Dick Williams Creek

•6233

Tonto

8000

5900

5800

Big Canyon

•6058

6200

6100

6000

5800

6000

Road

FR 29

6100

6000

Roberts   Mesa

5900

285

5900

Horton   Creek

5800

•5856

Creek

5700

5800

5746

5800

•5744

5600

5800

Turkey

5800

Horton Picnic Area
and TH Parking →   ← Upper Tonto
Campground

33

33

Ridge

5945

5800

FR 289

32

•5941

5600

5700

5900

6000

5800

5600

5500

Private Road

5900
6000
5700

new alignment and 4-laning planned

2002 alignment

•5510

Kohl's
Ranch
(all local roads
not shown)

5500

260

5600

5400

5600

**HIGHLINE 13:
Horton Creek**

0   1500   3000 Feet

0   1/2

contour interval 100 ft.   Miles

N

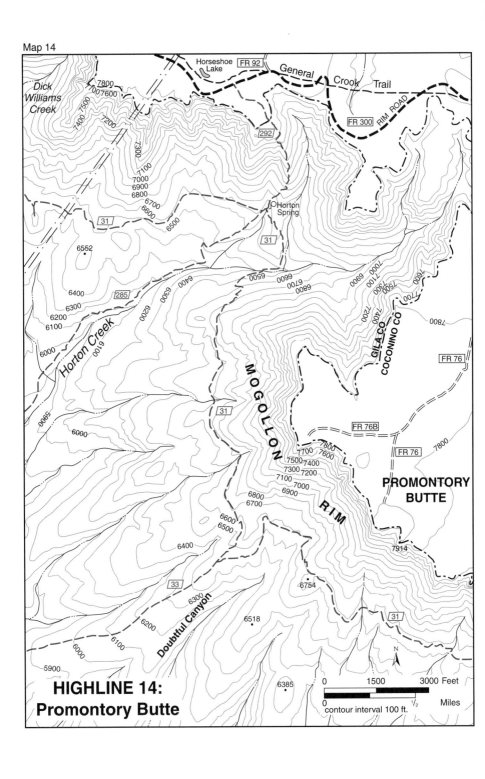

Map 14

Horseshoe Lake FR 92 General Crook Trail

FR 300 RIM ROAD

Dick Williams Creek

7800
7600
7500
7400
7200
7100
7000
6900
6800
6700
6600
6500

292

Horton Spring

31

31

6552

285

6400
6300
6200
6100
6000

Horton Creek

6600 6600
6700
6800
6900 7000
7100
7200
7300
7400
7500
7600
7700
7800

GILA CO
COCONINO CO

FR 76

FR 76B

FR 76

6000

7700
7800 7600
7500 7400
7300 7200
7100 7000
6900
6800
6700

M O G O L L O N

R I M

7800

PROMONTORY BUTTE

6600
6500

6400

7914

33

6300

6200

6754

6518

31

Doubtful Canyon

6100

6000

5900

6385

N

0   1500   3000 Feet

0   ½   Miles

contour interval 100 ft.

HIGHLINE 14:
Promontory Butte

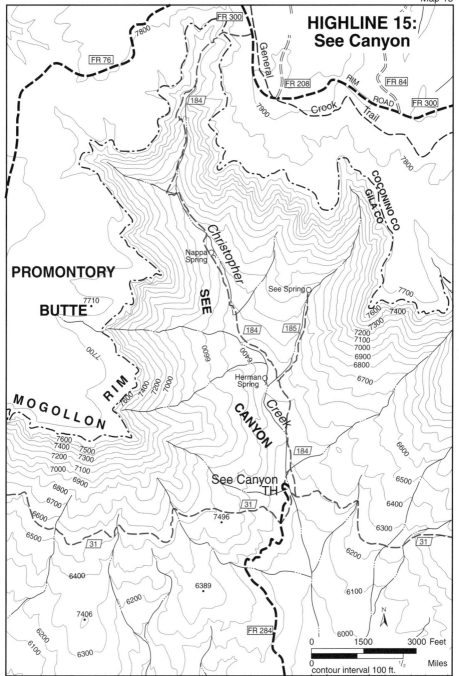

Map 15

HIGHLINE 15:
See Canyon

Map 16

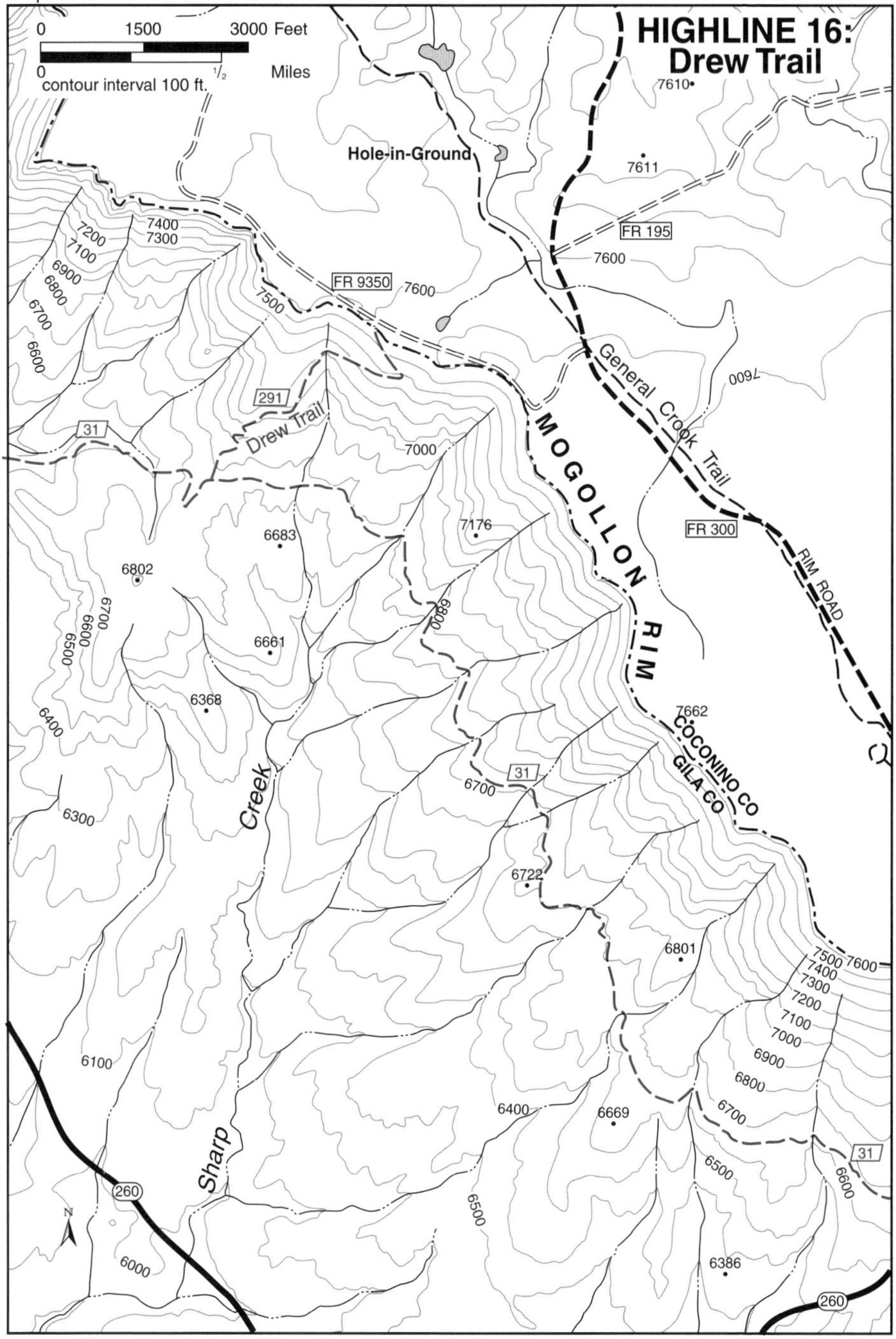

HIGHLINE 16:
Drew Trail

0   1500   3000 Feet

0 _____ 1/2   Miles
contour interval 100 ft.

Hole-in-Ground

7610•

7611•

FR 195

7600

7200
7100
7400
7300
6900
6800
6700
6600

FR 9350   7600

7500

General Creek Trail

7600

291

31   Drew Trail

7000

M O G O L L O N   R I M

FR 300

6683•

7176•

6802•

6700

RIM ROAD

6700
6600
6500
6400

6661•

6368•

6900

6300

7662•
COCONINO CO
GILA CO

31

6700

6722•

6801•

6100

6400•

6669•

7500 7600
7400
7300
7200
7100
7000
6900
6800
6700

6500

6600
31

Sharp   Creek

N

260

6000

6500•

6386•

260

Map 17

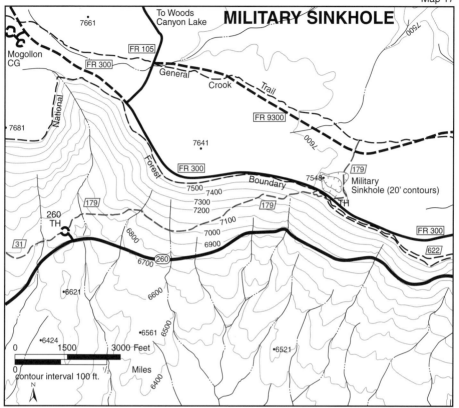

MILITARY SINKHOLE

To Woods
Canyon Lake

7661

FR 105

Mogollon
CG

FR 300

General Crook Trail

7681

National

FR 9300

7500

7600

7641

Forest

FR 300

Boundary

7548

179

7500

7400

Military
Sinkhole (20' contours)

179

TH

7300
7200

7100

179

260
TH

179

7000

6900

FR 300

31

6800

260

6700

6900

622

6621

6600

6500

0   1500   3000 Feet

6561

6400

6521

contour interval 100 ft.

Miles

N

Map 18

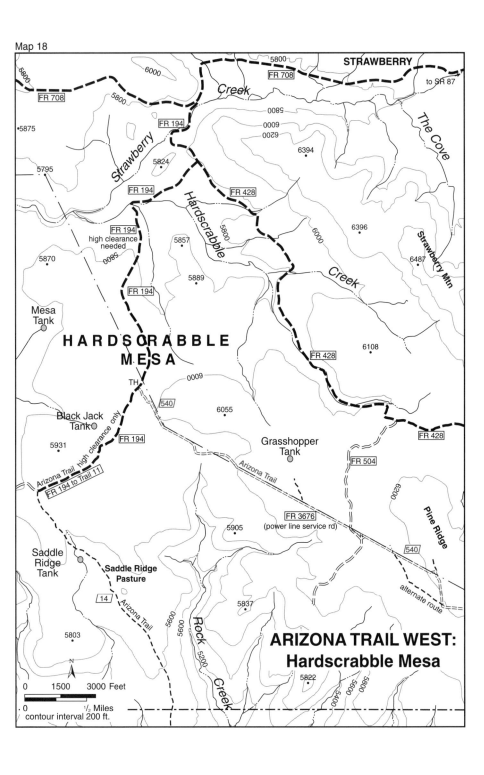

STRAWBERRY

to SR 87

FR 708

FR 708

Creek

The Cove

5800

5800

6000

6000

6200

5800

5875

FR 194

6394

Strawberry

5824

FR 194

FR 428

6396

Strawberry Mtn

6487

5795

FR 194
high clearance
needed

5857

5800

Hardscrabble

Creek

5870

5800

5889

6000

Mesa
Tank

6108

FR 428

**H A R D S C R A B B L E
M E S A**

TH

0009

540

6055

FR 428

Black Jack
Tank

high clearance only

FR 194

Grasshopper
Tank

FR 504

5931

6200

Arizona Trail

Arizona Trail

FR 194 to Trail 11

Pine Ridge

FR 3676
(power line service rd)

5905

540

Saddle
Ridge
Tank

Saddle Ridge
Pasture

alternate route

14

Arizona Trail

5837

5600

5600

5803

Rock

ARIZONA TRAIL WEST:
Hardscrabble Mesa

N

5200

5822

5800

5600

5400

0   1500   3000 Feet

Creek

0   ¹/₂ Miles
contour interval 200 ft.

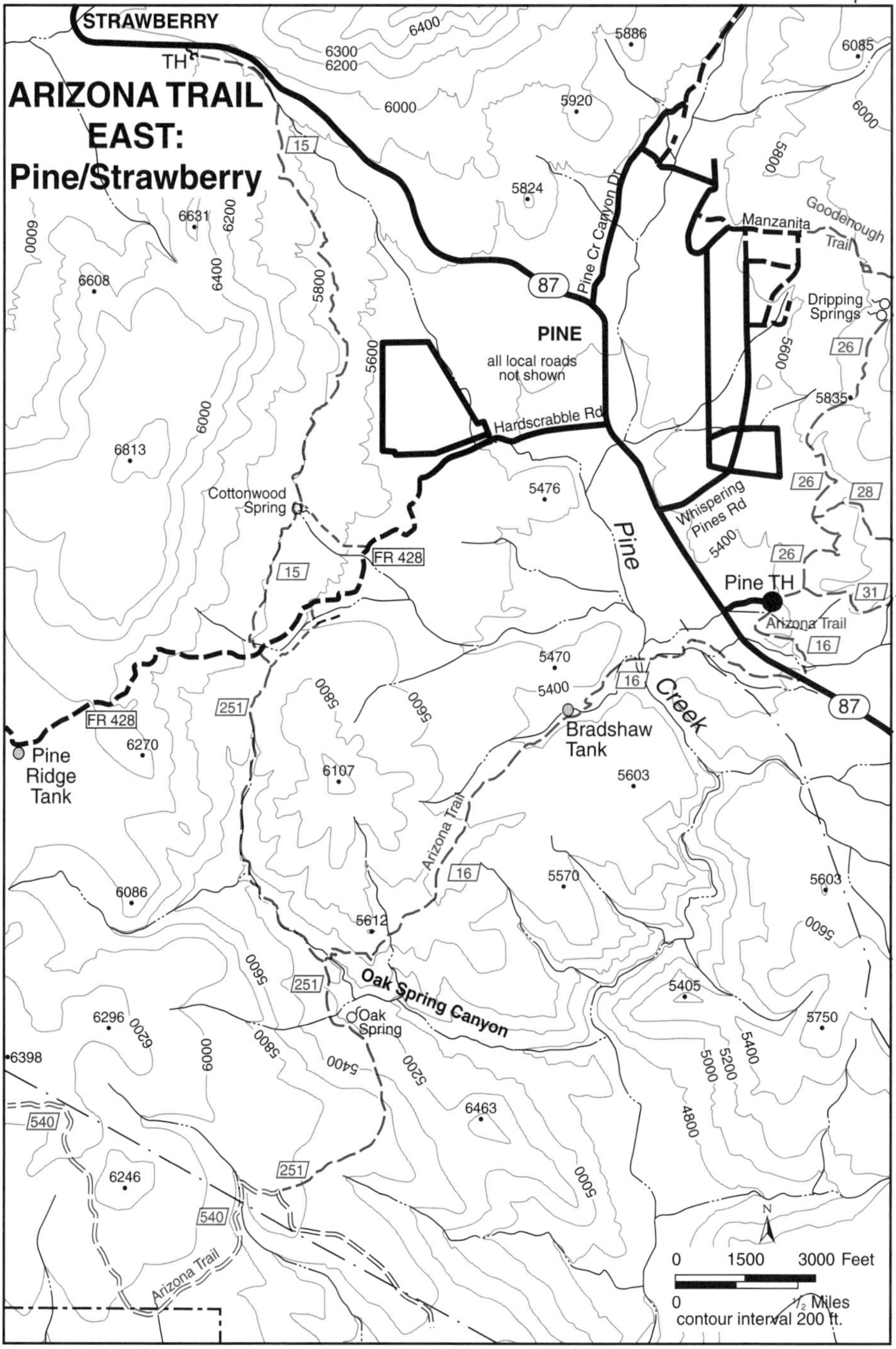

Map 19

STRAWBERRY

TH

ARIZONA TRAIL
EAST:
Pine/Strawberry

6400
6300
6200
6000
5886
6085
5920
6000
5824
5800
Goodenough Trail
Manzanita
6631
6200
6400
5800
Dripping Springs
6608
5600
26
5835
6813
PINE
all local roads
not shown
5600
Cottonwood Spring
Hardscrabble Rd
5476
26
28
FR 428
15
Whispering Pines Rd
5400
26
Pine
Pine TH
31
Arizona Trail
16
5470
16
87
251
5400
FR 428
5800
5600
Bradshaw Tank
6270
Pine Ridge Tank
6107
5603
6086
5800
5570
5603
5612
Arizona Trail
16
5800
5405
6296
6200
6000
5800
251
Oak Spring Canyon
5400
5200
5750
6398
Oak Spring
5400
5200
5000
6463
540
5000
4800
6246
5000
540
251
Arizona Trail

N

0   1500   3000 Feet

0   ½ Miles
contour interval 200 ft.

Map 20

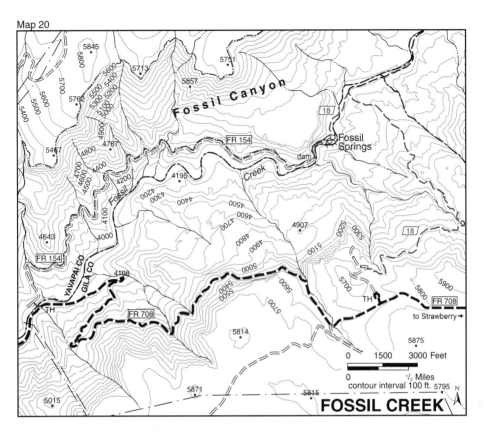

FOSSIL CREEK

Map 21

HOUSTON MESA

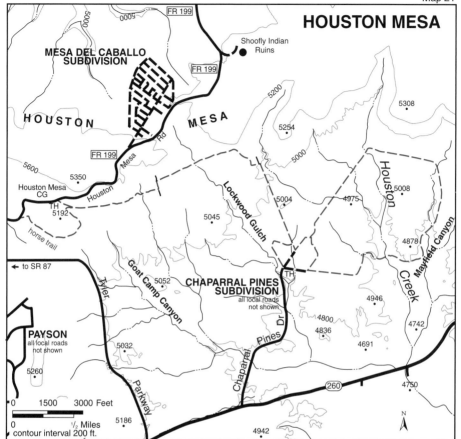

FR 199

Shoofly Indian
Ruins

MESA DEL CABALLO
SUBDIVISION

FR 199

5308

5200

H O U S T O N

M E S A

5254

5000

5000

5350

5600

Houston Mesa
CG

TH
5192

5045

5052

CHAPARRAL PINES
SUBDIVISION
all local roads
not shown

horse trail

to SR 87

Goat Camp Canyon

Tyler

PAYSON
all local roads
not shown

5032

5260

0   1500   3000 Feet

0   ½ Miles
contour interval 200 ft.

5186

Parkway

Chaparral Pines Dr.

Lockwood Gulch

5004

5004

4975

5008

Houston

Mayfield Canyon

4878

Creek

4946

4742

4800

4836

4691

4750

260

4942

N

Map 22

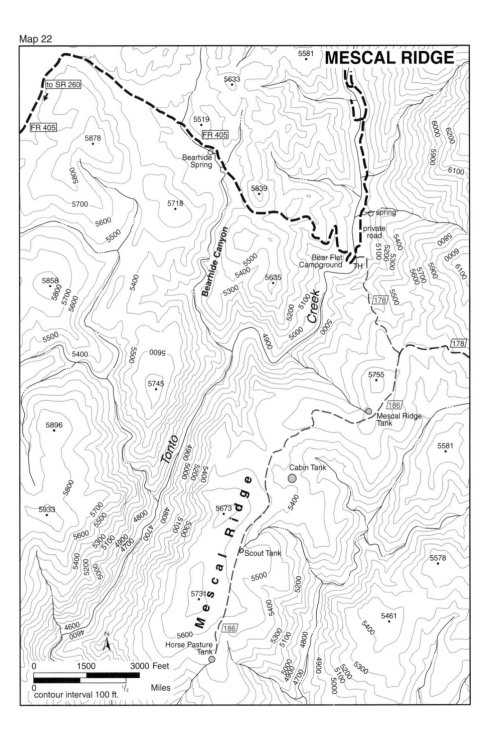

MESCAL RIDGE

to SR 260

FR 405

FR 405

Bearhide Spring

Bearhide Canyon

Bear Flat Campground

TH

spring

private road

178

178

Creek

Mescal Ridge Tank

186

Cabin Tank

5755

5581

Tonto

Mescal Ridge

Scout Tank

5578

5461

186

Horse Pasture Tank

0   1500   3000 Feet

0   1/2   Miles

contour interval 100 ft.

N

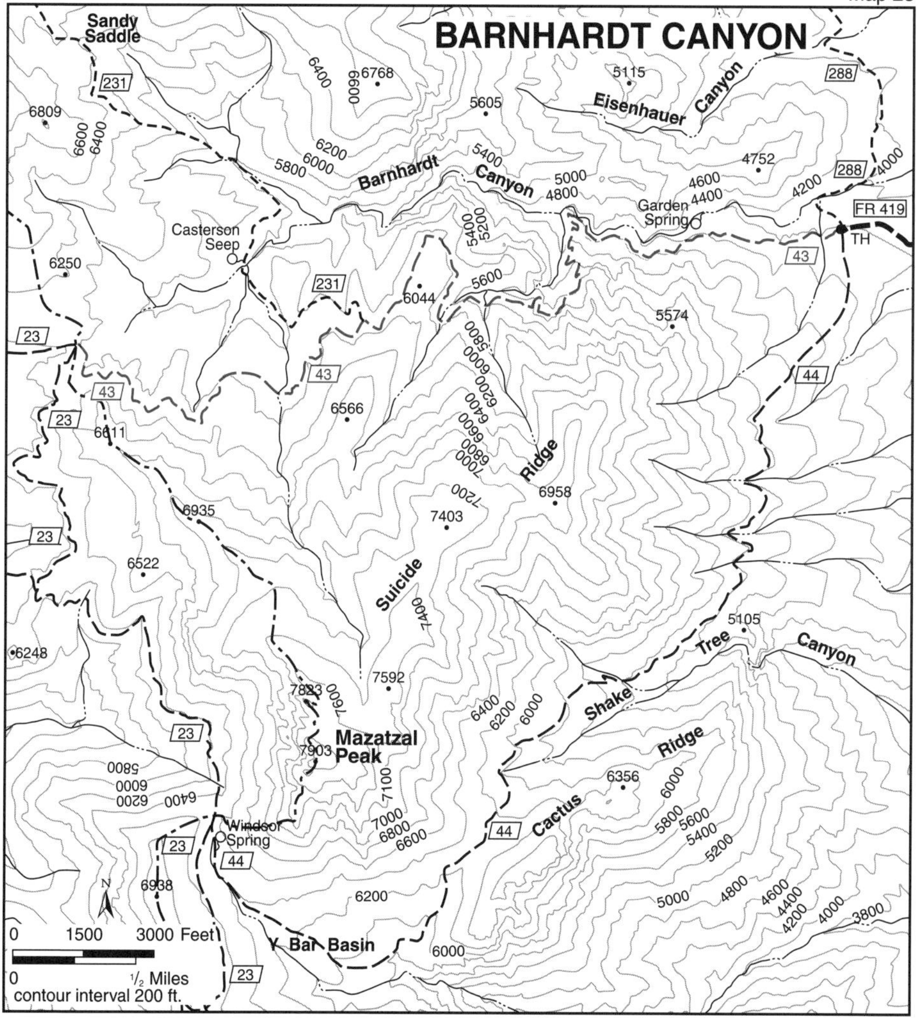

Map 23

BARNHARDT CANYON

Sandy Saddle

231

6809

6600
6400

6250

23

43

23

6611

231

Casterson Seep

43

6566

6935

23

6522

•6248

23

5800
6000
6200
6400

N

6938

0   1500   3000 Feet
0   ¹/₂ Miles
contour interval 200 ft.

23

Windsor Spring

23

44

Mazatzal Peak

7903

7833
7600

7592

Suicide

7400

7403

7200

6044

5600

6768
6600

6400

6200
6000
5800

Barnhardt

Canyon

5115

Eisenhauer Canyon

5605

5400

5000
4800

5400
5200

5200
5800
6000
6200
6400
6600
6800
7000

Ridge

6958

6400
6200
6000

Shake

Cactus

7000
6800
6600

7100

44

6200

Y Bar Basin

6000

4752

4600
4400

Garden
Spring

5574

5105

Tree

Canyon

6356

6000

5800
5600
5400
5200

5000   4800   4600
4400
4200
4000

3800

Ridge

288

288

4200

288

4000

FR 419
TH

43

44

Map 24

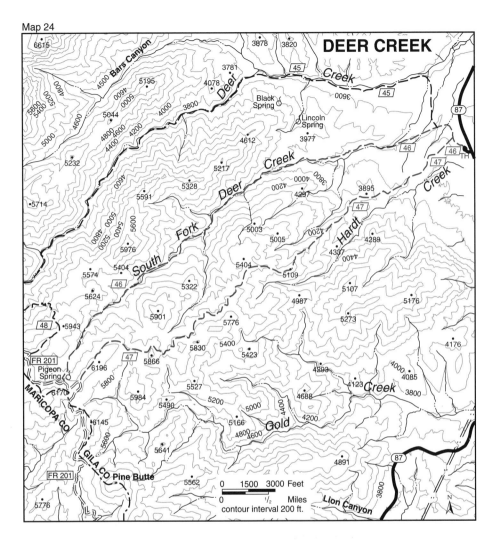

DEER CREEK

Black Spring
Lincoln Spring
Pigeon Spring
Pine Butte
Lion Canyon

Bars Canyon
Deer Creek
Deer Creek
South Fork
Hardt Creek
Gold Creek

FR 201
MARICOPA CO.
GILA CO.
FR 201

6615
3878 3820
3781
45
4078
5195
5044
5232
5714
5591
5328
5217
4612
3977
3600
45
87
46
46
47
TH
47
3895
4297
4200
4000
3800
4200
4400
4337
4289
5003
5005
5404
5109
5107
5176
4987
5273
5322
5624
5901
5574
5404
5976
5830
5776
5400
5423
4293
4123
4000
4085
3800
4688
5527
5984
5490
5866
6196
5800
6170
6145
5641
5562
5776
4200
5200
5166
5000
4800 4600
4400
4891
87
3800

48
46
47

4600 5000 4800 4400 4200 5400 5200 5000 4800 5400 5600 5200 5000 4800 4600 4800 5200 5400 5600 5000 4600 4500 5800 5600 5800

0   1500   3000 Feet
0   1/2   Miles
contour interval 200 ft.

N

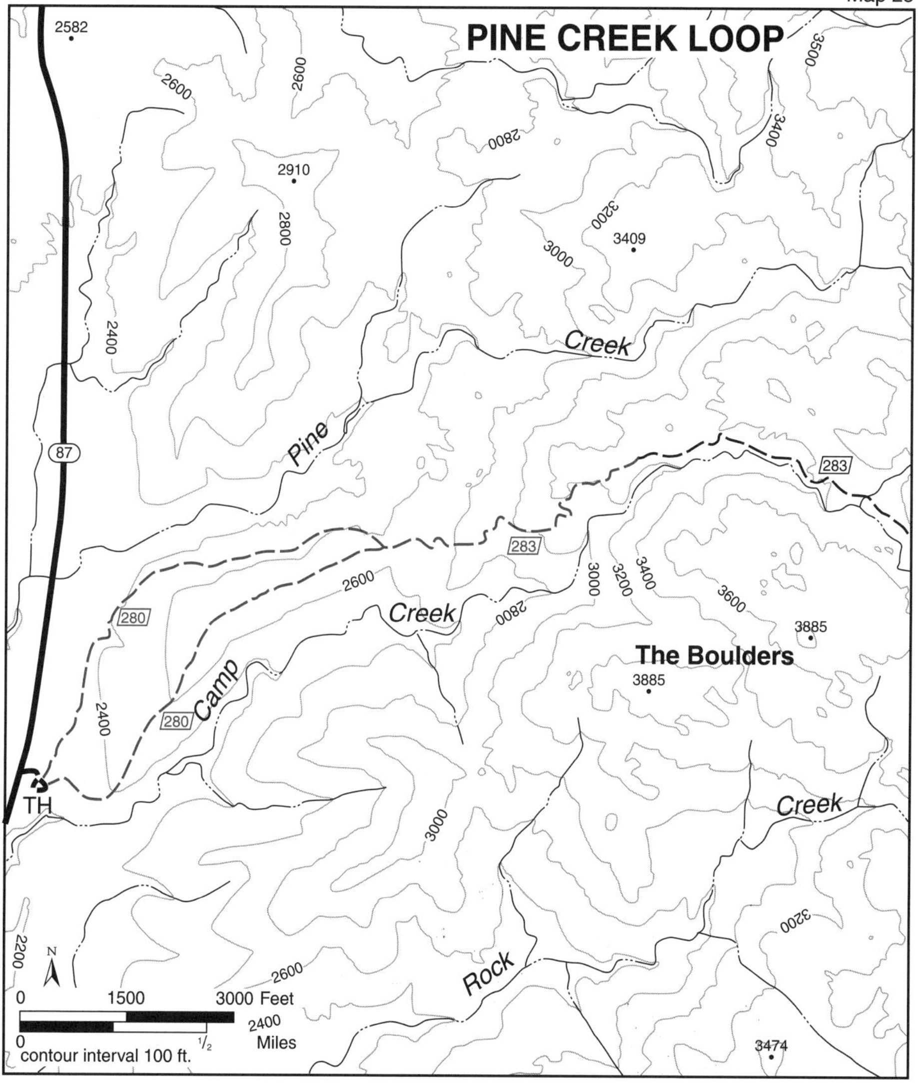

Map 25

PINE CREEK LOOP

2582

2600

2900

2800

2910

2800

3200

3409

3000

2400

Creek

Pine

87

283

283

280

2600

Creek

2800

3000

3200

3400

3600

3885

280

Camp

2400

280

The Boulders

3885

Creek

TH

3000

3200

2200

N

0   1500   3000 Feet

2400
Miles

0   1/2

2600

Rock

3474

contour interval 100 ft.

Miscellaneous Area Information

We have not attempted to describe all the other features of the Payson area. But there are a few facts that may be important to know, as well as some useful links.

Shoofly Ruins. The Native American archeological site is close and well worth visiting. It is no longer part of the trail system on Houston Mesa. Find it 1.5 miles east of SR 87, north of Payson, on the east side of Houston Mesa Road (see photo, page 120).

Tonto Natural Bridge State Park. We have not described this park in this book, but again, it's worth a visit. There are short trails that are unusual and heavily used by visitors. Find it north of town before you reach the Pine Trailhead, on the west side.

Local Amenities. Green Valley Park west of town (end of Main Street) is the location of the Rim Country Museum of the Northern Gila County Historical Society (www.rimcountrymuseums.org) and a small, beautiful artificial lake. On the grounds are the original Forest Service Ranger Station (1907) and the top of the Mt. Ord Fire Tower. The **Zane Grey Cabin replica** is being built (2005) in painstaking detail in the Park just east of the museum, by the Zane Grey Cabin Foundation whose Web site (www.zanegreycabin.org) has other useful links. There is a library at the museum and a public library in Payson, with many local books. The Pine-Strawberry Archeological and Historical Society operates a small museum in Pine (www.pinestrawhs.org). The Regional Chamber of Commerce covers Payson, Pine, Strawberry, Star Valley, and Christopher Creek (www.rimcountrychamber.com).

The Forest Service Payson District Office on the south side of SR 260, east of town, is a good place to visit for books, maps, and all the latest information _ especially important since the extensive fires of 2004. (Without their help, this book would not exist.)

Other Local Trails. Equestrian trails also suitable for hikers are being developed around Payson. Most of these are on nearby Tonto National Forest land, with public easements acquired for legal access.

The Gila County Trails Alliance (P.O. Box 695, Payson, AZ 85541) is a regional group of trail users that is helping in both trail maintenance and planning.

The Arizona Trail

Part of the nearly 800-mile Arizona Trail from Mexico to Utah is covered in this guidebook: east from Hardscrabble Mesa on Trail [504], via trails [251] and [16] to Pine Trailhead in 12.1 miles; then continuing on the Highline Trail and Col. Devin Trail [290] to the Rim in another 19.4 miles, for a total of 31.97 miles or 4% of the total length.

It would be remiss not to recognize the tremendous effort and dedication that has brought the dream and brain child of Dale Shewalter almost to fruition (except for 94 miles, as of early 2005). It is now developed and maintained by the Arizona Trail Association (P.O. Box 36736, Phoenix, AZ 85067-6736) www.aztrail.org. The organization has a Chief Trail Steward, local trail stewards, a Board of Directors, and publishes a regular and highly professional newsletter, *Arizona Trail NEWS*, and other interesting features on its Web site. This should be of interest to those enjoying the Highline Trail and other trails in this book.

For example, the Winter 2004 *NEWS* has color photos and stories about the trail work recently completed by the Arrowhead Wildlife Society on Hardscrabble Mesa.

- Notes -

- Notes -